✿

this
dedication
is for FREEDOM
for our freedom of

*E*xpres.**io**N

for our freedom of
ITs human heart
and for PEACE
to love and
let IT
be

✿

Keremeos, BC
page 42 #43 #(85)
Lisa Lewis

Published by:

FriesenPress

Suite 300 – 852 Fort Street
Victoria, BC, Canada V8W 1H8

www.friesenpress.com

Distributed to the trade by The
Ingram Book Company

...because of you, the mystery of life, of God, Spirit, Universe, All That Is, my heart feels. Family, friends, acquaintances, and those I come to know of outside of physical proximity have directly and profoundly influenced my thoughts and perceptions, my experiences. It is you who has so deeply touched my heart, and I feel grateful to share in this life with you THANK YOU your impressions inspire, lend strength and support in ways that speak through silence ~ ALL ANGELS ~ your support the gentle push when needed.

I had a wonderful experience with FriesenPress (thank you Megan, Izzy, Colin and Lynn). Their guidance, professionalism and spirited enthusiasm helped this process to be both educational and joyful, as did the women of JGBC, friends at C3T & Context International.

Bev (mom), Tom (dad), David (brother): None of these writings would have been possible without what each of you have taught me throughout my life. I love you with all of my heart.

Mitchell and Justin: You are both awesome and I love you!

Margaret and Janice: I love that both of you have come into my life, our family feels complete because of you.

Terry: Your kindness, strength and encouragement have helped me to realize my dream of writing. Thank you for all that you are, and all that you do. I love you, and thank you especially, for Calvin and Darby.

Catherine, Janet, Dave, Cathy, Michele, Julie, Colin and Heather: Your friendship, love and support means more to me than I am able to express. For all the times you listened during the process of this book, for believing in me and for so much more, thank you.

Mira, Aila, Craig, Seana, Lauren, Russell and Leia: I feel inspired by you, and fortunate, that you are a part of my life.

To the Wise Family, I am forever grateful. And I am grateful for him, from whom I learned about survival, forgiveness, persistence, resilience and hope. That when I feel faith, love resides, and when I feel blameful, overwhelm condemns in sweet voices. I have learned that my enemy is my teacher, too, if I am willing to explore, to welcome no condition upon arrival... and that life, is beautiful.

PROOF YOUR STAND

we may feel helpless at times
we may agree to believe that we are
and claim I alone can not and yet we must try
otherwise innocence becomes lost to complacency
birthing devastation in our wake
compassion feeble in attempt to renew

...HEART, lost in connection to emotional pain;
soul posts in need of contemplation;
engaging body-mind;
soul merging highest good;
yielding love's intention
and alongside humanities discrepancies toward NATURE
may we dehumanize to spiritualize
enough to forge balance
loss of LIFE not in vain, but for HONOR
MERCY called upon in our darkest hour
glimmering redemption; restoring faith; merciful
PROVOKE ME that I may flourish upon my flounder
unfurl in midst of coiling, spiraling upwards
amongst ourselves towards creation's haven
~ LOVE NOT ABANDONED ~
for waves of emotional torment
continue to fill the body with grief
life in the GULF suffering amidst selfish indignation
permission granted alongside our silence...
and I have heard rumor of my own insanity
because I cry myself to sleep at night
and burst in to fits of sadness in broad daylight
reach mute in longing
connection with those who dwell there
stemming from belly of earth

...PEACEFUL IN WRATH
rant randomly continuous
mind random in dreams
mind choosing conscious state:
ALIVE;

PROOF YOUR STAND

ABOUT THE AUTHOR

When I was nine years old I experienced a moment in time where I knew I was going to write. I was standing in my bedroom when all of a sudden I was struck with an overwhelming sensation that I was going to write a book. I scrambled around the room looking for a pen and paper. I draped myself overtop of a tall, five-drawer dresser and began to write. After a couple of sentences, I stopped. What I had written didn't feel right. I thought to myself "I am going to write a book and it's not right now". I put my pen down and ran outside to play.

During my teenage years I wrote poetry here and there, for friends and English class. There have been a few times throughout the years when I have tried to write in journals, though I never quite knew what to say – I would get a few sentences in, it wouldn't feel right so I would stop.

A few decades after that moment when I was nine years old proved to be my starting point. I once again found myself scrambling around the room looking for a pen and paper...I've been writing ever since.

Dance of the Starfish has led me on a quest to explore human emotion and the idea of a higher power, of Universal Energy; call it God, Universe, All That Is, other... there are many names for IT.

In this human form, life experience is my teacher, spirit is my guide. Animals and humans alike, my inspiration, and Peace, my motivation.

I Believe...
Passion leads.
Trust creates.
Faith becomes.
And that...

PEACE is possible.

L. Norris
www.peacejunky.ca

Starfish are amazing creatures. They are prolific, re-generative, fragile. As fast as they proliferate, they may be wiped out by toxic water. They sweep the bottom of sea-floors and exist in every major body of water on earth. They are graceful and precise and without a brain. Tube feet and a nervous system extending through their arms aid in the Sea Star's dance and navigation - gliding, sensing their way along.

Humans are also amazing creatures. They reproduce, some live many years while others depart swiftly. They have a nervous system with five tangible senses. Humans hold both incredible and undiscovered pow-ers of healing. They are both resilient and fragile, determined and fearful. They roam the earth's sur-face, infusing their will and might. They are kind and arrogant, nurturing and greedy. They inflict pain and suffering and create depths of love tremendous in strength when unconditional. Humans are conscious in ways seemingly different and unique from other living entities, elevated in both creation and evolutionary sense...

And are they? Unlike starfish, humans have a brain.

I wonder at times, if housing a brain makes a species better than, or above all in transcendence, choosing who shall live, or die; speaking for those who com-municate in ways unique from ones own.

I had a dream, that Starfish danced in their prolif-eration, born of humanities plight. And inside of my dream I woke up, to discover my dream had come true. That our brains no longer served essence, for greed had allowed it to gain control over emotion, over spirit moving through. Our common sense diminished by distraction.

The human entity; unspoken and as yet undreamt of potential awaits their arrival. And will they? Arrive?

Will you, will I?

And is not this what I desire?

To offer honesty in exchange for time spent shared and created together, each unit of flesh navigating home of God, Universe, All That Is, that we know of. And humanity; exquisitely flawed, our jagged heart edges saw through mire protecting our soft inner core where natural being compensates joy, and longing. Abundance born of sensory awareness; tuned to the unit; catapulting love, harboring sacred intention.

We all meander.

And at least as many humans on the planet, there are as many stars in our sky, stars in our waters, stars in the eyes of lovers. United. And for each shining star a dagger made of stones. The kind we throw. Separating. And just as starfish bake in the sun, darkness comes to guide us. To steal our souls, to suck us dry, to wash over us with madness. Temptation calls, filling soul with fervent denial; insanity displayed in our betrayals.

Stars surrounding us now.

Sister Ruby told of a tale. A tale of a boy who was walking a sandy beach, throwing starfish back to the tides. As he walked, and tossed, one starfish after another, the young boy was approached by an old man who said to him "Why do you bother, do you know how many starfish are littered on this beach? It won't make a difference". Without looking at the man the boy thoughtfully smiled, picked up a starfish and again, tossed it back into the water. Before moving on, the boy paused, gazed respectfully into the eyes of the old man and said, "I made a difference to that one."

God, Universe, All That is. Do I come, to know you? Do I look into eyes of another and discover? Do I care, enough to? And is not this what I crave? To be understood. To feel seen, be heard.

To love, and live freely.

LOVE
and speak freely ritual of being.
We have lived another life you and I.
I have seen it in your eyes,
felt you in my heart,
Deja Vu
(0)

.

.

.

.

.

᛭

THE GATE KEEPER

At heals of suffering beauty nips,
purchasing hope with light remnants,
bartering glorified dreams for sacred
intention; setting self-imposed limits
toward freedom. Suffering,
at hands of gate keeper.

precedence set me
FREE

᛭

.

.

. .

. .

We all have a story.

It has been said throughout time there are many paths on the roads we travel. It's a beautiful metaphor indicating freedom if we choose - that our actions build the life we lead, rather than circumstance dictating who we are.

And does it proceed the road we choose to follow directs us, we direct it, or we walk together as one unit; interpreting flow in communication between our body (physicality) and information (sensory data) streamlined through our brains via nervous system, through our human body adding to extension of mind? And do we live our interpretation of life, creating through action, and will to become? Do I carry fault, and what is fault anyhow?

I was reading the book 'Fault Lines' written by Nancy Huston, and it got me thinking. Perhaps a human fault line is where one erupts. Loses per-spective. Where one finds self out of control or in the perception of it - our lines crossing through migration in those we are closest to, the ones who receive our energy, and we receive from. Rubbing together causing friction, and growth, our evolution evident in mind now, compared to our history.

In case of life now what would our fault lines be? Is this our exploration, our expedition? To unravel our misdeeds in birth of awakening to po-tential? Perpetuating fault lines through waves of friction between us, a carrying of life forward by generation?

Our beauty sleeps to be awakened in potential. Individually we are spectacular in our gifts, our triumphs, our tribulation.

Where does focus live in life? Is it for a highest good? A highest disorder? A balance between the two where disputes exist upon which healthy resolution abides (life not taken for granted)? I believe there are supporters of all. In understanding do we contemplate in fairness?

Does equality exist as a template of being.

I was tried with a test of will, of personal strength; physically and emotionally. Body and mind exasperated. I had to make a choice. Would I stay? Continue in confinement of mind being held prisoner on outskirts of heart?

Would I choose death at the hands of my captor.

My name is Asil. Asil Sirron. We all have a story. Here's a glimpse into mine...

My captor wanted me to support him in suing our employer for treating us poorly (claims which bore no truth). He wanted to punish. Given my fear of my captor I concluded I had no choice - it's a scary place, living in a mind where believing in one's courage does not exist at a level able to secure physical safety for fear of being killed. A twisted place.

A long story shortened - our 'claim' required we

be examined by a medical doctor. We arrived at the hospital where we each had a doctor's appointment, or so I believed, he had not created an appointment for himself, he was using me as ammunition.

After my appointment was over, I waited outside for him to return to pick me up. He said he would be back in one hour. As time passed, I began to fear his return, and the state he would show up in. As he pulled up to the curb I felt anxious. As I entered the car, energy smacked me as if to say, "Here's an opportunity. Do not get into the car, pay attention to how this energy feels." It was the Universe trying to protect life, avert danger - my torment was thick.

I stepped into the car and we headed home. It would be a couple of hours on the road in dense, bumper to bumper traffic. I knew the choice I made would come to haunt me. I thought about running, opening my door and running. I chose to stay seated.

As we drove along air grew stifled, unavailable for relaxation. Under heavy weight I noticed my captor's face clenched in anger. His number one lead into physical abuse led by insecurity. He refused to believe my innocence at the hand of his accusations, he was beyond reason, obsessed in belief that I wanted to humiliate him, might I even talk with a man. He tried to make it true, to prove his misguided belief, his insecurity, his fear (the wearing of a blue, doctor's patient smock enough of an excuse to set his mind to rage).

In his mind I was guilty - nothing less than my

admittance would be acceptable. This was not the first time I had been in this place, feeling forced to admit to action that was not partaken on my behalf, but lived in his mind. One by one he started naming men that I had contact with, red in his certainty, black in his heart. He began to slam my head against the passenger door window. As cars drove by people stared into my world, looked into my pleading eyes and moved on pretending not to notice. It was then I realized he was visiting insanities lure, I his guest.

Between sobs of procrastination meant to buy time, I cowered in efforts to be heard, for my truth to be known, that I was not guilty of what he accused.

I wasn't meant to be heard. In a moment of silence where I felt time stand still, he looked at me and said, "I have no choice, I have to kill you. At the next exit I am pulling over, and I am going to kill you." An eerie calm replaced his anger, I searched for meaning - each moment a clue as to what would come next.

Suddenly, this life I had not paid attention to enough to keep safe, at once and in silence screamed for recognition, to help keep me alive.

We were driving on an eight lane highway, with edges of forest on our side of the road, rock walls on the other. As we pulled off of the highway and drove down the next exit, we sat in silence as we approached what seemed to be an ending, an ending of a life not yet lived in potential.

Our car was small on the inside, especially for a two hundred and sixty pound body builder - a mass of muscle wigged out on some kind of endorphin rush coupled with the beer he had been drinking at the bar he went to while waiting to pick me up from the doctor's appointment.

As he slowly rolled the car to a stop at the end of the road, the scene from my view was a flash of familiarity. It was a typical scene where dead bodies are found - a treed area where passersby cannot, or do not see in, the perpetrated stabbed with anxious resignation, so close and yet so far. He turned the car off, and for a few moments no words were exchanged. And then, the line of questioning resumed, "I'll give you one last opportunity to come clean, to admit to the offenses I accuse you of." Even then, knowing my life was about to be over, I could not bring myself to abandon the only thing I had left, my truth.

He started counting to ten and before reaching its duration - madness piercing his glaze, beads of sweat profusely exhibited on a curtain of hatred, bulging shame - his face exclaimed descent into darkness. Within moments he clutched at my chest as he lifted and heaved me into position, facing him, my back pressed hard against the steering wheel he grabbed a large chunk of what little hair I had left, as much had fallen out stressed, and smashed my head into the windshield, cracking the glass. With his hands clasped around my throat, pressure created in the small space we inhabited threatened to cut off my life, and he did, proceed to choke life from my body.

I struggled, and writhed for breath. Eventually, as life in my body grew weak, I recognized panic's futility, serving no purpose but to weaken my spirit and feed his rage. So I stopped fighting. I accepted my position. Death was visiting at the hands of my tormentor, my torment fulfilled in extreme. As physical life meandered in the distance, leaves gently dancing in rhythm, mind kept me company and spirit graced my heart. As consciousness slipped, my life began to 'pass before my eyes', it was a feeling that encompassed every life that had touched my own.

Every one was there; an instant that held no measure of time and so is forever. In those moments of instance, mind turned black while faces of people in my life whom I loved very much, appeared together, floating in space.

My sight landed upon my mother's face and waves of sadness enveloped me in the knowledge that the next time she saw me it would be in my death. The emotion so overwhelmed me, she gave me strength, her spirit pure with love. In those moments I decided though my tormentor was taking my life, that if I was going to die, I was going to die with a smile on my face, that he could not take away what belonged to me in truth, an inherent ability to choose how I wanted to feel. In those last moments, I chose peace. I curled upwards the corners of my mouth, until I felt my body smile, and I surrendered, accepted my plight and fully let go of my physical body. My arms limped to stillness as my body relaxed in the bliss my mind endeavored.

I died.

That was then. A story from another time, and we all have a story. What tale do we tell? What life do we weave upon telling? To what does Rhythm of Heart flow...

In temptation to take action putting off my dreams for one more day, distracting myself in less than par commitment to start living my dreams now, a voice from my head started speaking through my lips, and this is what the voice sounded like "If you are wanting to make a change happen in your life, you must take action now. There is no other time but where you are right now. In putting your dreams off until tomorrow, you are using your time creating action that you do not desire, doing so out of habit or obligation. Start to create your dreams right now, or wait until forever comes and you will be found to have spent your whole life dreaming about what could have been. When purpose knocks at the door to your heart know it is love; let it in...and then, spread your joy."

You, me and Sister Ruby. Our difference existing only in our expressions of how we each experience our birthright to life. Every day Ruby asks me, "What exactly are you doing to make your dreams come true? What are you doing to become the most fulfilled human you can become?" That voice in my head, the one that told me to let love in, that voice belonged to Ruby. In essence, Ruby sought to know of heart, to understand it in other people, to feel, and become heart's rhythm.

I liked to play the devil's advocate with Ruby and I would suggest to her, that it has nothing to do with heart, that there's a part inside each of us that longs to let go, yet holds mighty in fight closing mind to bodies purpose, becoming numb in the process. Physically unable to feel, much. More criticism and greed really, satisfied in by-product of heart's non-participation, feeling unmotivated, cranky. Ions agitated in stagnated state, burning our cells within cancerous rage, and other ailments. We are how we feel, we become what we think and what we choose to consume. That in-between lives interpretation. Our expression by way of our senses: what we see, hear, touch, taste, smell are cumulative chemical responses. A building of memory; a production of history. Each moment ahead new. Each memory lingering - choice to become, standing middle ground.

I would ask of Ruby, how many addictions (memories relied upon?) may one body house. We all eat and drink ourselves to death in the end as the masses presently believe our plight to be. Some paths shorter, some longer. As we exert less vital energy body gives way to source; calling spirit home, to engage - ashes of flesh returned to material source.

And amidst my playing adversary, I realized, it was

myself feeling deprived. Strangely displaced, mis-placed, disconnected, lost in illusion of time.

Ruby would say that when we know who we are we quit fighting.

I have to ask why in the past I have given love away in receipt of no return. Was I unable to receive? Was I disarming others from giving love's gift? An inability to witness? To take stalk. Dare I heighten emotion in giving energy of love through touch, and all sense...

And Ruby, Ruby fought to become who she is now. She was consumed with internal battle between knowing what feels balanced, and taking action from there, or being drawn to heightened emotional reaction to surroundings contributing to high or low body frequency, one emotion at a time; difference occurring between the shift. I'd often find Ruby in a daze. I would taunt Ruby and say to her, "Is this where we live? Stuck in-between what we know, swarming; blinded, and with our backs turned?" "You are beautifully cynical" Ruby would tease, and would then share further perspective with me, in writing.

Following is one of the first writings Ruby shared with me, she wrote:

When we experience events and everyday interactions we create in our lives for what they truly are, without adding emotional satisfaction and description,

when we recognize reaction and choose
response, we then exist in the present
and may continue to create our next
current moments in truth. Upon removing
emotional reaction to our manifest,
to interaction endeavored, we create
opportunity to experience being;
one's emotional response
born of love's guidance;
to experience ourselves
for who we are in the moments we choose
the external world we create to bare no
controls upon us. In the removal of
emotional reaction we release binding
energy patterns created by our
thoughts, and experiences, and, we
shift our experiences in life from
those of external description to that
of internal knowing; experiencing what
there is to know in each current moment
interpreting flow - our search, and
discovery revealed of which we truly
are, blossoms. Our truth, I believe,
is essence of All That Is,
and is what nurtures our personal power
within our system of Humanity.

As we come to know our essence,
we become aware of and experience our
already enlightened being. I believe
in this life it is through our
intellect, and love, that beings may
share 'light'. That through the
sharing of our intellect,

consciousness, faith, and intuition;
guided by spirit, we may discern our
personal truth and share the light
within us, with others.

Our intellect, our consciousness,
our faith, our intuition, are all but
finite parts of the infinite - they are
tools bestowed upon humans, along with
desire, imagination and expectancy,
that make the journey toward
the experience/attainment of unity
recognizable, understandable, and
ultimately achievable, each one of us
a benefit, and gift to the WHOLE...
...creating change without violence.

(3)

I used to wonder, if Ruby was describing physical and mental adaptation toward focus. And I wondered if Ruby shared her thoughts in writing because she felt the most at home there, the most alive and peaceful. I suppose I must as well, be the most comfortable in my own thoughts - for whose else thoughts can I be but my own interpretation?

I enjoyed receiving notes and letters from Ruby, she would place them conspicuously in curious places. I feel her words on the page, and her obsession with writing often creeps into my dreams.

Ruby is my twin. She spins long, dark, thick threads of hair, her eyes green as emeralds which sparkle and dance in the light they emit. Love surrounds Ruby's life, as though it lives inside of her, as though bursting to seep through her pores. Her naivety at times astonish my fear full heart.

Inside my own imagination I've slept on hell's doorstep and hung in its hallways, begging for entry. It wasn't my turn. I am grateful.

Ruby and I have led very different lives.

We were born in a village amongst friends, and strangers; those not yet met, and somehow, curiously, I felt known - as though anything hidden was seen by those silent around us, our essence flowing freely in the ether that surrounded, and supported us. Presence we feel. Presence we are.

Ruby and I - twins in heart born of one - at times emotional conspirators, at others emotional opposites. Always connected. Seeking. Questioning. Pondering love moments and tribulation.

Ruby's heart shared with me, that she had come to believe her tendency toward extremism had been trying to tell her all along that life is interesting, that life is meant to be stretched in order for it to grow. She believed that every possibility lives inside of heart, inside of mind, existing, waiting to be plucked by desire born of love. She had come to experience emotion impostors, posing, bearing witness to lies told to herself, of who she thought she was. And in relationship to that which is occurring now, Ruby believed, that every emotion acknowledged within acceptance expands in creation of itself as truth develops core.

Above all else, deep within Ruby's heart, she believed within humanity lives desire to become humane.

Ruby would often say to me, Asil, why are we here? Her question was never meant to be answered, but rather pondered at great lengths.

I tend toward thoughts of our history being our truth, no matter how much our memory of it changes, no matter what our personal understanding of it is, it is what we make it. Each of us acting as one, and together. And do we recognize each other? In recognition giving acknowledgement so that others may receive, for who or what else will give?

Our village was vibrantly perched, and nestled, amongst rolling grassy hills with meadows that glowed in their stunning example of life, living with color - its vibrancy matched by the hearts it procured. Leaves became greener, flowers brighter, and all things touched by love came alive with light and beauty, expanding in silence.

Yet in the background, beyond the safety of the grassy knolls, darkness hovered, expanding into depths unknown. The villagers did not dare to explore it. Elders warned of impending doom to those who risked the travel - that temptation stole minds willing to wander. And tales were told of an old man, who to this day walks the shores of a distant sea, heart caught in bitter memories of a time where the darkness swallowed him whole, as yet not able to free his soul. And it is told that a boy was sent to save him, to bring him home.

Ruby claims she ventured beyond the safety of our village in a dream. That the atmosphere was magical, peaceful, rooted in basic human need; survival. That lush forests amongst mystical spaces sit adorned with mists of time: haunting in beauty amidst its captor; darkened heart, where plundering flights of flurried rage bestow in victims mind. That merciless in hunt, the darkness rummages earth to ravage flesh and steal our souls. Yet wondrous sights restore balance keeping our sanity whole, fed, nurtured by mother earth; recognition of love's endurance. Ruby said spirit told her that all have right to life, to free expression of it, that receipt of personal injury will become abandoned in love's abide.

I have not yet told Ruby of my secret, it tears at the fabric of my being. And it, too, is a story for another time. Right now? It is morning, and soul awakens to all love in the world, seeking place amongst its creation; to become what it is. And as earth's breath longs to be received, winds howl in their gifting; life, settling in for the day.

Calvin finds the most comfortable spot in the house, in his mind ? the fluffy dense pillows of a wine colored love seat, and while snuggled in, his anticipation of breakfast is contained just enough to not be driven into madness; his morning ritual.

Darby sits patiently, waiting for the next cuddle,

wishing for love's touch above all else; love sustaining her. And breakfast bubbles on the stove top longing to nourish those who will partake. What exchanges dance on the edge of days unfolding?

Today, Ruby and I acknowledge our birth day, our time accrued in measurement of our physical bodies ability to continue in growth, spirit residing. "Ruby, where are you when I need you!" Ruby often disappears on birthdays and holidays, leaving me to represent, to partake in the festivities life hands down through ritual; at times awareness that possibility exists to try something different becomes lost on me. "Ruby!" She has no doubt disappeared for the day.

"Darby, your breakfast is ready." Calvin is already waiting. I enjoy when life cooperates toward accomplishing a goal. Though I can attest it happens less than I would like to experience. I can hear Ruby in my head, telling me if I truly want to experience cooperation that I will need to cooperate.....speaking of which, "Darby! Your breakfast is ready!" Reluctantly, Darby makes her way while in search of love's expression, gently taunting patterns of chaos by feeding them bits of her soul.

After indoor festivities? Adventure! Calvin, Darby, myself and hopefully Ruby will head out to explore the mystical meadows (and perhaps beyond). In the meantime, I'd like to share some of Ruby's letters with you. I've been collecting them, and have numbered and organized them in this book. I've added sporadic commentary and thought ramblings in hopes that you will too, as there is room throughout for addition.

Ruby's writings are prose to ponder. Random in order, they are seeds, of contemplation...

...blemished bliss and random rants;
there are humans in our midst.
And love and hate are one,
connected in tendrils of heart
we grow. We are all of Us.

What story do you tell?

CAUTION
Some of the writings in this collection may be
'grammatically not correct'.
If temptation leads to seek grammatical
correctness within traditional form,
let go;
read within flow

.
  .
   .
   .
   .
  .
  .
 .
 .
 .
.   .   .
.   .
 .   .
  . .
  . .
  .
  .
  .

WOMB OF SOUL
In womb of soul
love dances as it is.
And as we grow in emulation,
breath; becomes conscience,
heart; conscious.
(58)

Mind
our greatest illusion
and
of mind results energy waves of
spirit moving through; spirit-energy:
its pathways lead into flesh of body,
and as received we vibrate sound that
energy creates.
As body experiences change in energy,
it adjusts itself at energy motional,
(e-motional) levels in order it may
balance itself with purest combination
of energy possible in moment it exists,
to coexist in harmony.
Brain interprets emotion through our
nerve receptor system, and a human body
creates sound to emulate energetic
communication.
Brain interprets sensory stimulation
upon adaptation to external stimuli…
body responds, we interact, we become
perception, we apply influence.
Mind
spins out of control believing it is in
charge. Emotions Speak; heart center
is focus of core,where soul guides,
spirit lives and God creates;
conscience.
Speak it as you feel it,
Tweak it as you be it.

Conscious

EMOTIONALLY TRANSLATED
While holding life energy at core
distant to other thought form
and mind holding intellectual focus,
energetic self occurred;
connected by perimeter,
creating energetic interaction;
remaining close to home
in authenticity.
Within authenticity
audible vibration expands
simultaneous with depth
and growth of feeling;
love watered.

Feel through vibration
of hearing,
and hear.

Feel through vibration
of seeing,
and see.

Feel with every body part
and every body function,
and upon so what does one feel,
and become,
when emotionally translated?

Fortified awareness filtered
through thought implied action
healing templates of being?
(38)

Is one's life as great a gesture
as one's manifest intention reveals?
Of what do we detail?
The moments we grieve?
The moments we dream?
The moments in which we are,
to live conscious birth each moment
wrapped in current being,
expressing in exchange;
true nature driving potential
as a parting into whole being
and so it is;
in the becoming
(60)

**Is it possible? For humanity and all that is,
to be encompassed and expand within harmonies
consumption...**

The other half of infinity will
continue to expand as we seek to
discover that which we do not know,
creating life in process.
Heart, leading us home.
(61)

RECIPIENT VISION

Dare we leave love, to come back in
its own time - not amplified
in vain?

Temptations sway.

That I will burst in the insanity of
this moment in time where denial of
self promotes extracted vision, of
who I am, and long to become.

Explored in nonsexual way?

Recipient vision. Acceptance. And
in receipt become whole in body,
spacious in mind, open in heart
- within each other.

Fluid in love's incantation.

And inside partitions of life;
rounded and scuffed, jagged and
smooth - we turmoil amongst it all
in the furnace of earth's atmosphere.
Growing until heat disappears
with no more fuel to burn.

Is the money worth it?

(80)

Energy teaching essence, guiding
to love unconditionally. In presence
no temptation to defense. Of its
receipt are we meant to share
in what is learned, to journey with
others in life - a truth quest? In
sharing essence, do we come to know,
having given permission to do so?
Mind minding body-body minding mind.
BODY TRAINING MIND THROUGH FEELING.
(74)

Evolutional Creationism

Creative Conscience? Is there such a thing? When we cease toward particular action, offering no energy, no life force as exhibited through the human body as expression of the idea in contemplation, are we free to choose our next move? Is result of paying attention to emotion what becomes physically - mind creating in its moment of conscience?

Does changing our mind toward what we want require physical response relative to vibration of thought-form moving through body, and complemented without distraction?

When a physical body is home to toxins, does our ability to know what our emotional, and so physical needs are, regarding action on human be-half?

There lives drudgery in sludge that toxins create; holding static energy in area of body where energy is traveling through. Our physical and emotional body becoming ill, emotionally unstable, moody: losing energetic power with which to concentrate, experiencing loss of patience, our bodies feeling irritated under stress of toxic buildup.

Do animals in the wild die of cancer.

Does energetic vibration received from spirit become misinterpreted as our mind-body connection becomes unclear; its transmission misunderstood in translation, the original intention of spirit diluted relative to ability to physically process?

We consume toxins into our bodies by way of the air we breathe, the food we eat, the water we drink, with what comes into contact with our skin, and in reaction to negative thoughts we think.

Does thought originate from spirit-energy? Creating life form of the earth?

Clean water, clean nutrition: clean communication?

I wonder, do animals suffer on our behalf? Their awareness pure, and in love choosing to take on our misdeeds in forms of suffering, to help heal our selfish wounds?

How can I bear it if it's true? Calvin and Darby companions of heart, extensions of soul, recently diagnosed with cancer.

...Planting seeds for future growth,
at some point harvesting now;
suspending intellect
to integrate heart
flowing as emotion,
separate and at once;
congruent in body-thought
to intellect.
(81)

In purity we are given life. In
deviation, do we pursue loss of memory
of who we are and where we come
from? Why does memory fade with the
increase of years? In order to
remember who we are, and why we were
born, are we to learn how to induce
memory of stored body emotion during
those first years of unconscious
remembering? As it seems now,
becoming whole in knowledge of
existence, our consciousness of
source fades of its own identity and
we become welcomed to the world we
live in, in order we may love it in
return, replenishing source,
and energy; growing life:
one at a time we reconcile.
(96)

Ohhh, Calvin and Darby, did I steal your life energies by asking for your love? As I speak this question I feel selfish, for my heart knows you gave freely. Does guilt chain my soul?

What may I claim in knowledge but of my own experience? How I experience God, Universe, All That Is, who I am, what I believe, what I create alongside created, what I recognize through observation of others, of myself. Judgement least desirous of nature? Advantageous in revelation? And what of judgement? Self-assessing behavior of another's offering relative to own emotive reaction, seeking control outside of acceptance, does meaning of judgment not also belong to my own being? When standing in judgement are we far enough from awareness to dwell in vision of separate nature? Allowing us to discriminate? Does love overrule and forgive us our trespass, allowing room for our hearts to grow and minds to gather wisdom in our lack of it? Self deception a slippery slope in human transaction...how often does one fall? How often does one rise?

Mind, our greatest illusion? Body, our soul deception? Projection expanding from core all that we think we are, existing outside of ourselves - seeking what was left behind; essence. And while feeling external from core we procreate and come to fear ourselves. And we love. Love remnants of creation? Evolutional Creationist - Creational Evolutionist. Semantics. Is it not all the same in the end? Paths differ, what is remains no matter our description of it. Emotional Pervasion.

True for one, true for all;
in breath we share creation.
Each moment simultaneous,
equivalent in growth;
life preceding itself in flow.
Being happy; being sad.
Being joy; being sorrow.
Each unknown within absence of other
=
recognition required
into opening of mind full heart,
and heart full mind.

Each emotion: energy-motion:
expressing itself in time
with existence now.
Energy moves us.
What does it mean in mind
how does it feel in body?

Regardless, we are one of all of us.
And at point in self-conscience,
soul expands being into the world,
self-conscience becoming one
with all that is accepted;
becoming brilliance
in brilliant being.
(97)

Dare I contain breath long enough
to feel and become rhythm of your
heart, touched by love, knowing
peace. And may all burden you bare
become my burden, your weight in
sorrow brightened by love's
intention. And may love pour through
others in order you may receive it,
and shine...and there is sorrow to be
sure, it lives alongside love,
scribed in castle walls amongst
dimly lit halls. And outside,
freshly adorned moon beams its
light energy, feeding our souls with
joy - sunshine running through our
veins. Sorrow a part, joy its
reflection. Connected by breath,
in tune with heart direction;
Dare I.
(95)

The human vehicle: a vehicle through
which to fine-tune. The only time
you have is right in front of you.
We can't touch tomorrow, we can
watch it grow. Upon our choices.
We can look back, to remember what
we have become by who we thought we
were...and then, we become our next
thoughts. And here we are, in this
moment together. My thoughts
written on this page and you reading
them. Welcome...
(135)

In placing mind to follow emotional
observation toward a present moment,
do we solicit life prematurely in
the anticipating of future manifest
outcome. By emotionally reacting to
that which represents possibility of
projected outcome, though is not yet
formed in present; and becoming
manifest as thoughts progress it do
we determine our energy motional;
(e-motional) existence in realms of
illusory measure? Within
observation of energy now, and
following its flow with integrally
focussed manifest action, one
becomes in natural flow - truthful
representation of one's being.
(110)

What does one do, if taught how to think and not
feel? For hatred needs only for us to think about
it. The deed done. Energy creates varied action.
Does thinking lead to killing? Does Heart lead to
Love? Think about a red dress on a purple mon-
key holding yellow roses and how this image feels.
Chosen thought pools of energy drawn to us caught
by our attention, creating development. Who am I?
Who are you? Energy beings creating light born
of recess past. Why does anger draw vengeance?
Why does love create more love? Why do Calvin and
Darby consume my heart so?

LOVE; Beyond measure…
Energy of Love amasses greatest
measure of unknown, and is All in
its wait of discovery. IT clings to
us, wanting to penetrate skin
through breath, longing to sing
in the talking. Does one abide?
Does one accept? Is one aware?
In ITs desire do we push it away,
intention not owned;
bearing deflection in our souls.
Do we eat ourselves alive?
Do we nurture that which grows?
Do we sit with Peace?
(4)

Someone close to me asked what my
desires in life are, so I asked myself
that same question. My thoughts began
to contemplate love, and I began to
feel, and then thought;

A degree of love, whether negatively
or positively vibed, shows itself with
each interaction known, and is capable
of enhancing growth of love worldwide;
the scale of love's vibration ripe with

opportunity to be nourished by heart
– yet heaviness falls upon us, a
suffocating blanket I imagine the earth
feels with every bit more of material
goods we put on it, taking from it.

My wish is to give the world as much
love as possible, inspiring more love
to spiral onward, upward. At times
I feel so high on life, in connection,
that when I come back down in
vibration, I must once more get
to know myself, crowded in self doubt.
And in our offering earth as much love
as possible, will our children,
and their children survive?

And love, is the quickest path to
feeling good. Love carries us when
we cannot emotionally feel it in our
highest sense - rather shows in the
depths of anger and blame, whether cast
or cast upon. Love tempts us to laugh;
inward and outward. And it propels us
forward in lightness of being, our
essence catching wind of humanity;
a representative species.

How do we reside?
To what does spirit call home?
How do we react, or respond to the day
we find ourselves surrounded in?
In search for growth of love I wish
to feel the emotional pain which

accompanies a new discovery of self,
that moment of letting go as a result
of a completion of understanding of
that being held onto; that feeling of
being moved to a point of expulsion;
where understanding, delivers dilemma
to be one with the rest that is
accepted - to feel emotional ecstasy
which accompanies higher choice.

Love moves soul and delivers mind in
quest of understanding being.

Soul longs to express truth as a
personal identity; a universal base
infused through mind to body - spirit
dancing in and through interpretation.

I am human, a carrier of dark, a
servant to love; writing. In my most
desired dream, world peace moves from
concept to manifest while in this human
form I am able to see, and feel, that
which we have created as one
- an unconditional moment in time
where in unison, we, a human race,
feel the earth's sigh of relief,
precipitated by our love toward her.

Sitting, with Peace.
(1)

(2)

It has been a long while, that I have
felt as though my heart and mind will
explode; their relationship separate in
efforts to be individual, one over the
other as if opposed to one together; a
battle proportioned in life over death,
love over hate, peace over war, you
over me, me, over you, and joy over
sorrow - a battle of polarities,
suffering in silence.

And yet, in a turning of tides
I recognize, embrace, and experience
depths of joy in recognition of sorrow;
a release; bridging gaps in dualistic
mind, for duality exists only within
containment that mind creates.

I have come to believe it is as one
soul we breathe, that in each breath we
represent all. That in light we love,
and while in dark,
we simply feel love less.

I have come to know my greatest sorrows
as revered joys, and my greatest
torments as cherished accomplishments,
for they are equal in love and in
merit; and are disguised as difference
which dissolves in wake to similarity.

And yet, so long as humanity holds
belief in duality, peace will remain
unearthed as war will remain its
opposite, while supported, in belief of
disconnect. And still, in consideration
of all, love remains; duality becoming
remnants in the wind as humanities
conscience comes to recognize itself...

...and blame gave itself, to consume freedom from
choice. In loss of itself, choice became motivated
by observation; acknowledged self defeatist. And
as war rages to protect insecurity, loss of power
gains false fulfillment in bullying, and forced con-
trol. Taking with blatant ammunition, speaking
to it in guise. Action speaks louder than words.
Denial fools. War continues...

...And in wake of discovery that we are
meant to trust our heart and live
amongst leaps of faith, that we are
meant to believe in our dreams enough
to take action, with heart playing lead
role, an offering of ourselves,
in love as we feel it;
One Soul...
May I offer the following ode...

❀

ODE TO LOVE
Love is a journey
in midst of its own existence.
Love has no boundaries
or issues of time
it has no 'beginning'
it has no 'end'
and love exists, waiting,
for us to discover its essence,
our essence;
to choose to be on its path.
Love is pure, simple, kind, sweet,
passionate, giving, receiving,
peace full;
it is the journey of one's spirit
in connection to one's soul,
in connection to soul of another.
One Soul.
Love flies through depths of being,
having no limitations,
no place in bondage.
Love is energy waiting to be freed.
Love is eternal.
Love has no beginning;
love has no end.
Simply, Love is.
(21)

❀

My love does not love me. Or perhaps my
love loves me in a way I do not accept,
so reject.   There was a being in love
with life. Enough so to love itself,
community not in way. Exception one.
 A controller patroller - one whose
watch patrolled their intimate partner
in hopes of finding oneself, somehow,
amongst jealousy, and denial. Denial
of unknown truth; unaware. And jeal-
ousy, jealously stealing core of self
and other, a byproduct of mistrust. And
in mistrust carried forward, swaying to
music that does not belong, nor adjust,
 are wild and crazy hearts dancing in
fire of pain. There was a being, whose
exception buried love within self pity
 and righteous indignation, blind in
sight. There was also a place, a place
were believers swelled in rapture, joy-
ous in their midst. Happy. In love;
trusting. This is what she feared.
Coming to know animal being. Her self
that longs in craving for love's puri-
ty, and opening...and in fear of self,
 do we replace trust with blame? And
when we are not projecting responsibil-
ity do we allow rarity of love to shine
 forth through chorus of heart. Full
circle when joined with another in more
than it is previous, and upon accep-
tance of itself, growth not thwarted?
There was a place where every charac-
ter was full with passion; vibrancy

lucid, and with zero objective save
for heart's expansion. Zero Objective.
Enough to expand on. Mind status; ec-
static communication observation; we
receive, endless, until consumed. And
until then, life. Call it as sensed.
Be it as received. I thought I was
afraid to share it with others, now I
know I was afraid to share in it my-
self, in the divine beauty I see each
time I interact with another living
being. We are full with love. Create.
Take action. How can we possibly know
who we are one moment from now as it
does not yet exist but for mind's pre-
diction. Too far ahead, and so we
starve in our hunger, killing ourselves
as we bloom. If we are one, my truth
is your truth and we are; blended in-
dividuality. There was a being in
love with life. Enough so to love it-
self, and share that self with others.
(107)

**I wonder if when Ruby wrote this passage, if she
was thinking about one in particular? Was it about
herself, was it about me? Could it be you, or another?**

**And Ruby, how do I come to know mystery while
consuming soul nature, depleting resource from deep
within belly of fear. Shocking waves, exploding
tremors. Longing to break free...**

Emotional breakdown?

We all experience them, at different
times and with different rates of
aggression. 'Time' spent in trivial
matter, vain in attempt of seeking;
external in decision making,
led by material stimulation.
Material Stimulation;
desire manipulating forms of life
with seemingly 'lesser' value than
our own and placed as greater value
than highest common good;
taking from the earth
without replenishment;
creating chaos as her power
is much greater than our own.
Do we think we can outsmart
that which feeds us?
Is it about you versing me,
or me you? Is it about
living together, sustaining life?
Ability to do so becomes a game of
dominoes as life in the Gulf meets
its peril, divinely inspired food
source succumbing, life beyond
plants continuing to fail in what
they receive from us.
GET INVOLVED.
Take action.
Our governments are taking
liberties of control.
As is sense of entitlement.
(123)

Our life mosaic changes as our
energetic values are trusted, their
appearance an everyday miracle; where
human creation is experienced as power
beyond the human body, seemingly
separate though support is all around.
And perhaps support shows itself
through 'human' animal, 'pet' animal,
'wild' animal, and through spiritual,
vegetable, mineral and gaseous matter,
the winds that blow, the air we
breathe. Do we honor support by a life
taken for granted? Do we recognize
support in order to know honor? Must
one sift through selfish nature to
understand what giving implies? Do all
of us, here on this planet we agree to
call earth, need to process emotion for
what it is to aid in soul maturity in
order to become aware of, and then
receive heart's guidance? Learning our
way by paying attention to how body
emotions feel in the moments they
occur, to name IT, call it for what it
is so we may create the Peace we
say we want? How else can we get to
know it, and grow it, if we do no not
pay attention to Peace becoming a part
of who we are? Is who we are
where we put our attention; emotional
congruency? At all times we are
supported. And when we hold expectation
of someone else's energy to feed us,
when we cannot muster enough life

energy on our own – do we, may we,
become synonymous with that of Integral
Nature; subliminal support helping
to keep us whole?
(141)

Sometimes I think I understand Ruby, and resonate
with what she writes, at times I need to write my
own thoughts, for clarity to come:

I BELIEVE that Unconditional Love is Natures
Aphrodisiac, that presence of nature inspires us to
feel unconditional, and that we are here, on earth,
for the nurturing of what we inspire in each other.
That Love's abundance guides us All, that awareness
of Love in our life experience shapes the life we
lead, the radiance we emit, and the compassionate
strength that we are.

I BELIEVE when I lack awareness of my physical
expression of body, acting on action born mainly of
thought; heart not consulted, that I suppress emo-
tion in miscellaneous regard by lack of acknowledg-
ing what is emotionally impeccable within my being.
What is true to Energy Motional Being in magnitude
of moment is cumulative action toward purpose,
each one's flavor becoming complete, enhancing
representative Nature of being one of the whole,
disintegrating concept of separateness, feeling one
in and with life's connection, All supporting All.

I BELIEVE that in focusing awareness inward we
are naturally drawn in desire toward elimination of

toxic mind buildup in our being; a freeing of mind creating clarity in that which was perceived as negatively charged - now supported in unconditional love; peace full intention growing pursuit of Peace.

I BELIEVE world suppression is on its way out. That negative energy gives its rapid display of life more so as it feels, and experiences its death. I feel it every day, that Love is more powerful than any other emotion; Love propagates life and negative energy is life's 'ego', and we are, upon awareness, servants to Love, redeeming Nature.

I BELIEVE that anything is possible, especially harmonious being, alongside our ability to become peaceful humans. If I stop placing excuses in the path of integral honor, will I become more responsible in the letting go of a need to suppress what holds truth in intuitive perception?

I BELIEVE mercy resolves peace.

Worry breaks trust, its energy

creating action of interference.
Interference creating chaos survived
fear - promoting fearful existence.
Chaos by design.
Altered in mind control.
(15)

THE REAPING

LOVE. Love is our greatest ally,
becoming foe while tempted inside of
fear. We seek and follows reaping.
And do we become older alongside fear's
embrace? Wiser in our acknowledgement
of it - something greater than we are?
And our fear is great.
Greater than love? Can we deny either?
Would they exist
without prompting each other?
And what of all we reap?
Who am I, who are you,
what of all of us in this moment?
What we feel we express,
whether aware of its essence,
or twisted in subliminal tendency
- expression is of itself; truthful
amongst our misconceptions.
So many layers on which we feed
in denial of ourselves.
Is being of ourselves how a body
transmutes interpretation of life
source? 'Energy' most commonly
referred to as what we name God?
And name IT as we shall
- holding responsibility
to action born of it.
Heart determines action.
Action determines heart.
Image is not real
and yet guidance lives there,
speaking to us
through silence of itself,

our condition in life
unto that we choose.
Love not conditional
upon choosing so...
(85)

I am sitting here with Calvin and Darby, and I have been thinking, about energy. How it moves, and shapes us. How we talk about it, deny and accept it - is there a place in energy where the center of all being exists, the starting point radiating outward in growth, in determination to live, propagated in love; shared in compassion and selfless in greed...does a place exist where love without condition exists?

Animals are full with free expression, no conditions, no emotional attachment holding back love's desire to be held, embraced in its beauty and promoted because it is in the highest good; promoting justice.

Ruby and I were driving home one night, the road 'dawnish'; enough light to be regarded as so, yet on edge of losing itself - this is when deer come out to graze alongside our converted earth, too many road kill. I am guessing the car in front of us, the one glimpsed around corners, must have been the one to experience the hit. As we drove nearer, I noticed the deer still moving, unable to support itself. We pulled over, though not for a couple hundred feet as I was struggling with the thought of dealing with the pain of loss it conjured. Ruby was powerful in her request to support humane action.

I parked, and as we ran toward the deer, a car driving by on the highway slowed to my pace and through an open window called out, "Asil don't, you will get too upset". I stopped inside of myself, questioned my action and turned and faced to walk back to my car, and, when the passerby was out of sights, energy moved me to return to what Ruby and I had set out to do: be in tune with the unit in those precious moments of fear.

This beautiful creature's gaze fearfully explored our presence. We sat beside her, holding one hand on her heart, one on the back of her neck, and did not say anything. We sat with her in silence.

Another woman stopped her car, crossing the road to be with us. Eventually, the deer calmed, it seemed her spirit had conquered fear.

...about 2am that night, Ruby woke with these words streaming through her heart, she felt it was the deer speaking through her;

Earth angels, in form of women, held
my last breaths in their hearts.
Through spirit, in form of these
words, I wish to express my love and
the love of every animal regardless
of the pain and suffering inflicted
upon us by humans. We are here on
this earth to remind human kind how
to love unconditionally, as love in

purity is what we offer. My appeal,
as I lay in abandonment, dying from
impact of human interaction, is that
each human moves toward holding
emotional responsibility for action
partaken that harms life. We do not
blame; rather, we encourage heart
space to open in these moments, our
hope and faith toward love's
encouragement. And of my remaining
breath, these words I offer to the
human responsible for the impact of
physical pain and loss of life on
earth; animal spirit now surrounds
you in unconditional love, sharing
with you what we did not share
together in those tender and raw
moments, in hopes that you will feel
moved to love more, and fear less;
to feel humanely inspired.
Unintended infliction of pain
occurs. And, upon occasion where
fear directed action results pain
upon any life form, I ask you to
consider the meaning the words of my
last breaths whispered invites; to
choose compassion, and trust over
fear, and know; spirit will continue
to massage your heart with love in
reflection of love's intention. Our
physical deaths sharing opportunity
in honoring life's blessing; that of
love. Be in peace as we are.
(39)

Do I stand in judgement
when I sit here offering merit to
but one perspective? Does not each
as well hold within itself its
opposite, its outermost reach from
what it is now and amongst all its
in-betweens? Opposites grounding
purpose within range of all
opportunity. Each to be respected,
all managed within love's intention.
(72)

Trust means that I am going to
do my part with or without wait-
ing for another to come through
first. (Do we impose greater than
our share, and share enough?) If
you were your goal met, what
combined set of actions play out the
meeting of your goal? Are those
actions ones that you want, and
trust, being responsible for the
life you direct one step ahead, one
step behind, one step where in
entirety life is itself? Do you
undeniably love what your actions
are and to where it is they lead
you? For what are you grateful, and
what do you desire to be grateful
towards? If you were your goal met,
how would you want to be able to
describe your journey? Do you meet
yourself along the way?
(22)

Love with all of your heart, that
which you plan to let go. If
connection is lost, release it, set
it free, it deserves to become whole
in itself. Do we hold each other
from love in claim of loving
another, demerits upon soul
capturing heart's attention, wishing
we were elsewhere in our lives. Who
we spend time with. Who we love.

Who we play with and make love to.
Do we honor another in holding
onto connection overdrawn; drive to
move on in pursuit of love for life
becoming perpetual motion,
acknowledged.

For what is as
exquisite as loving yourself in
recognition of another? You move
me. Bits of yourself honor my
essence and in its receipt I become
whole; with spirit - seeing,
feeling, experiencing parts of
myself only visible through
interpretation of another; who you
are. A blessing. A gift of soul
great enough to propel my love
seeking heart. Love in all measure,
setting us free from ourselves.
Acknowledged acceptance driving
our lives in purpose; Love.

(94)

Ruby, I have come to believe that as humanimals we experience spiritual relationship with everything animate and inanimate, being we are spirit. Our spirit/soul, both essence of same, directs and moves our physical body. Our physical body establishes and directs itself, in order it maintain relationship with mind, and within its own identity, in order it may respond to mind's request. in addition to its own. Awareness of the workings of what one's brain produces in communication from the mind to the body and the body back to the mind essential. Mind and body experience a state of being stuck by repeating the same behavior over and over again, without new emotional (spiritual) energies in application of the behavior, without renewed inspiration.

We are equipped to know everything there is to know now, as it occurs in relationship to everyone and everything around us, within any given moment of life experience. Through ego-mind we build material world. In awareness of mind/body transmittance, we experience our actions for their truest energy being generated, clarity gaining ground regarding truth of our own energy output, whether 'positive' or 'negative', free's emotional burdens we carry. With indomitable spirit generating mind; purity of heart calls us home.

Recognizing ourselves in others, and others in ourselves it is our deflection of reflection that harbors our grief. How we describe details of life, whether they are about ourselves, or others, is an expression of our own mind reality in any given moment animated through the human body. Or, could it be a combination of energies forming mind's reference. Minglings of mind.

In bringing awareness of bodies vibe to the place where energy of recognition resides, and by investigating the action our mind/body connection manifests, we invigorate mind; capturing nothing, expressing all — life moments; do we taste all the ingredients we throw into the bowl as one unique flavor, and savor each in turn? Am I asking you or trying to sort myself out? Am I insane? Are we all, insane in some degree? It is a question I visit. How far in mind do we travel, extending our vision of self...so far as to kill each other...so far to agree with it...so far as to love freely? I wonder, will I serve my next moment within dark, within light? Does emotion one feels result of energy moving through body by sensory adaptation? Is soul everything animate and inanimate? Does soul know everything and everything know soul?

As humans, do we experience our intellect taking control over the meaning of our emotions? When we use our intuition are we being guided by our soul mind in clear communication based upon feeling; mind following guidance of spirit, producing action born of divine flow, no unsupported energy attachments to figure out and let go of as we move the energy through our physical body by way of accepting the energy, lending support and removing density of 'pain'. Energy of pain becoming lighter in weight, becoming more and more 'enlightened'? When we respond to our intuition do we experience balance in body-mind communication?

As animals, do we connect through heart center?
Is this why Calvin and Darby have been here, as
a part of my existence, to teach me of heart and
warn me of mind? Ruby, have I done them justice
while they have been here? Did I love them com-
pletely? Fill their hearts? Is it even possible, to
fill another with love...must it be chosen?

I am not sure that I am worthy,
and that's not to say I am not,
for who am I to judge?
There is chaos and order.
Order we choose, chaos we navigate;
Beings in Universe.
as pixels on the page we flow together
(168)

IDENTITY
As it was, as it is,
as it shall become;
our lives intertwined
in mass of identity,
all but one to claim.
(92)

Shifts in Perspective
Association: everything learned.

If my association with heart
proves me vulnerable,
Am I weak in mind?

If my association with heart
proves me paying attention,
Am I true?

Ecstatic Communication;
Primal Association.

How does sharing associate
self-centeredness?
(75)

Intuition reveals all there is to know
relevant and sufficient to the moment
we are moving into and through.
Passage from entrance to exit of a
moment may become stuck in negative
energy pattern; emotions entering into
a moment may not be free to exit. The
more moments we experience energy being
held within our body - those energies
of anger, frustration, fear, depression;
the more stifled life flow becomes
through our being; the reliving of
these energies cause blockage in our
bodies. Do we relive energy patterns
when we do not accept life
occurrences for what they are?

A stifled being lives in scarcity on
some level as ability to open to life's
flow and gifts that come of flow become
squandered by holding emotional pain
within our being, within our waking
moments. An act of holding energy is
to withdraw; a holding life force
captive in attempts to control it,
'thinking' we will succeed in our
desires. These held energy blocks
'burn' the human body, causing
heaviness of spirit, decay and
dis-ease, the energy too dense to hold
in a human container for great lengths
of time without mutation of the area
where this energy is being stored
in the body. Energy is meant to flow.
To heal one's body, become aware of and
then change patterns of negative
thought that one dwells on.
By insurgence of positive energy
into one's body,
created by developing inspired
thought patterns, we heal the body as
there is a constant flow of life's
creative energy through our being,
our human nature.

Divine flow is a human cleansing
system. Positive energy flow demands
free expression of it, its movement
flowing in tune with Divine Timing.
(16)

Times I feel unhappy are times I force
myself to be something I am not.
Discontent brews in repeated feelings
of failure, of not living up to ideals
that do not belong to me and yet
maintain presence, ones I do not
innately understand and continue to
hold long after they were given. And
what is true begs to be discovered
amongst the fallen, and fortunate.
Does searching outside of self discover
vacancy of heart, sadness of soul,
anxiety of mind? Distracted in fantasy
- stories told to others and so of
self. And in love do we honor our
greatness? Do we allow it to touch our
minds, to seek our soul upon spirit
flow...In love does wonder share its
stimulus offered in feelings of
happiness, joy, trust? An all
knowing sensation in thought,
of heart's rhythm,
in tune with the unit. One with
another. Voice cries out in the
bravery, of soul spilling through.
Sweetness lingers. Love bursts.
Desire claims want in connection.
Unity. Physical union blowing mind
out of proportion in order to fully
enter heart of soul, to propagate love.
(109)

Our lost connection?

Does Emotional Literacy speak to that
which causes loss of and through
physical awareness; emotional habit?

...reacting ahead of time to a
preconceived notion intellectually
driving our emotions instead of waiting
for truth to spring forth from them???

(surrender to emotion and have faith)

Meaning comes.

I imagine 'doors to heaven' cannot open
when we do not provide it with
connection it recognizes...ones through
heart center, and mind center (mind
without extraordinary control), both
heart and mind working together.
(101)

**Life is like being tickled by millions of deep fuchsia
colored velvety translucent bubbles, floating along
runway toward higher ground, while on a level,
shimmering way through hexagon sunbeams in mind.
What ghastly beautiful horizon beams ahead — to
only discover more beauty? Ah; the love; I have
reached playground; starry night and bright light
take me Om.**

DOES SOUL KNOW MY NAME?

Natural in beauty we flourish until,
human experience grows larger
in mind than heart.

And how to sway into balance?
Become what we once were...
child like in heart
while maturing in mind...
exuberance for life not changing
while ever-changing perspective
leaves us new.

Connected.

In heart I know sadness, and joy,
anger and love, betrayal and trust.
I know humiliation and blame,
humility and innocence.

Love tempts,
provides natural balance.
Daren't to indulge...

I wonder,
does Soul know my name?

(108)

Upon moving through the world amongst
our fellow beings, endeavor to take
each step with an open mind and willing
heart. When we feel ourselves
responding to someone or something with
what feels like judgment - delve deep
into our core, open our hearts and our
minds, allowing judgment and fear of
that which we choose to not understand
to be replaced with acceptance, and
further call upon courage to emulate,
by way of our very existence,
the creative mind within which
we all thrive.
Are we not all but expressions of one?
Seek to discover within emotions we
manifest and of those expressions those
we experience harmony with;
and choose to live there,
and grow from there; touching all who
come to visit the home within our being
with grace, dignity, respect, complete
and full acceptance. Understanding and
growing in tune with the underlying
nature of those we encounter on our
paths, discovering our true nature
through illusion of separateness. And
in separateness we find our way back to
oneness by contemplating how to once
again become personally whole.
By looking inward at our outward
expressions, we encourage discovery of
the meanings behind our actions,
that what we see in others is

reflection of our own nature in
particular regard;
our emotional creations.
Embrace each journey fully,
within its own merit, letting go,
giving way to expansion.
(17)

The smaller the life force
the less communication with it?
The grandeur one's heart imposes
offering spirit
in recognized capacity
omnipotence revealed in time.
Mission to seek its meaning,
illumined in heart filled desire.
(90)

**In Being, do we chemically change mind in midst
of adaptation. That we may adapt that which we
choose - our bodily actions.**

Does freedom lay in ability
to remain in focus at depths
of ability allowing mind to be
free of inconsequential chatter?
And freedom(?) is not something that
a political party can represent or
government declare, nor found in
whimsical notion - rather in
achievement of heart's intention, a
giving up of mind's control in order
heart may dictate routine in trust,
within integrity.
(79)

Ruby would often say to me, "Be it as you feel it. Tweak it as you speak it." Being twins she knew when my mind was taking over my heart. She could feel it in emotional distance I created between myself and others. I did not create this distance with her, nor with Calvin and Darby. All three of them felt as extensions of my personal being, perhaps our love for each other complete...

What one feels energetically within
one's body, that is of nature; is of

being recognition-ally enhanced, is
being upon spawn of innate desire
to express truth filled passion
propelled by action. 'Our' action,
as each interaction within
atmosphere of molecular love creates
only itself and sets opportunity for
more of next action, cumulates by
way of life energy; a flowing of
source. Energy motion of love, as
well as hate, requires reciprocation
of own to survive. Humans are meant
to reciprocate birth in love from
within; deteriorating hate away from
source. How deep does one feel
inside one's energy motion? How
far does one travel on filaments of
thought in mind? Energy-motion
creates thought, and thought floats
naked until gifted with feeling;
conscious focus of moment
experienced. Emotion and thought
combined in harmony, in acceptance
of the other, blending balance of
body, mind and spirit creating
energy motion within unity; a gift
of being; timelessness. Love is
grandeur to hate. Love can, love
does, and love is enhancing the
world. To live within reciprocity
of love: illumines peace in core,
and peace, on its way home,
lights being.
(36)

What about our sixth sense?

Ruby and I go back and forth with different ideas about it. Perhaps, when fully engaged, our sixth lends ability to experience our tangible sensory receptors in as grand of an expanded form as is possible within our minds eye in any given moment. How do we experience Nature? How do we experience life? Do we experience these things through our five senses in the human body; sight, hearing, touch, smell, taste? Vision, sound, feeling, absorption, embodiment.

Is ability to experience any one of these five senses to its fullest extent within one's mind proportional to one's own spiritual development at any one time? And available, and achievable through a conscious act of single-pointed focus; divine connection brought into awareness - a mingling of all energy. All that is and is not yet in our awareness being of it? Anger and other negatively charged emotions are manifest projections; existing outside of being as attempts to release misunderstood energy moving through.

And in our defense do we speak hurtful tones, to keep ourselves, others, and the world in which we live under our illusory control?

Spirit nature is unique within each of our expressions of it, yet is it common underneath manifest projections? Look inward for guidance in all matters of life and feel personal truth: speak it, feel it, breathe it, live it, be it, desire and hold space for it to arrive, and peace will come home. Reside within. Coming to know essence of being. Acceptance of all; changing that which is out of integrity into emotional congruity. Do any of these expressions hold validity?

Does truth show in the becoming?

As though in taunting mind roams freely
- dropping hints and handfuls
of pleasure, tastings and blasts
of truth, while lacing perimeter of
consciousness with the human condition,
a field day of maneuvers in which one
swims and drowns, drowns and swims;
entertaining rebirth of yet another
layer to be reminded of the layers
within each; questioning knowledge of
seemingly unknown nature, yet all told
defers to awareness in state of being.

To what do we succumb?

In our greatest form - LOVE
and in love's purity;
vibration...maneuvers born in fear
of unknown giving way.
(12)

Anguished Euphoria, bits and spurts.
As I was wondering about ways to
eliminate relationship, nostalgic
knowing locked itself inside of heart,
tempting chase while in reach for joy.
What? I do this?
Allow experience of past to dictate my
future, holding onto emotions
I have no control over?
Wonder permeates clear recollection
born of all that is; all-sharing
center; moments of connection.
(159)

Do we experience the energy we refer to
as love to the depths we allow
ourselves to experience the cognizant
receiving of it? The strength of love
energy we feel toward a particular
moment reflective in how much
acceptance we feel within that moment,
and within non-acceptance, repel it -
such as the brushing away of a bug that
has 'landed' uninvited into our
personal space - the brushing away a
'knee jerk' reaction to that which has
touched us, deflecting out of fear; we
'push' love away from our being,
holding ourselves in patterns we have
developed in reactions to protecting
ourselves from that which we do not
understand? It feels as though energy
of love is based in acceptance and
within acceptance what more is there to
know, than energy of moments endeavor?
(10)

DISTRACTED RITUAL
Born into sanction for participation
in organization of humanities greed,
distracted in ritual.
Loves sets us free.
(160)

Is there anything as great as fear
to bring us to our roots?
(104)

❀

VIBE

A stand in vibe adjusts itself to
root...while in root,
nourishment proclaimed.

A stand in vibe promotes itself in
cause...while in cause,
action warranted.

A stand in vibe becomes itself.
while itself,
Trusted.
(66)

(161)
SOULLESS KEEPERS AND HEARTFELT SOULS
No one is home at the doors of Saint
Peter's, he's bringing his cows home to
milk. And when Reaper gets way,
shouting ***chagrin**, do we dive in
and tag soulless keeper;
offering love's disrepair?

*chagrin
annoyance, irritation, vexation, exasperation, displeasure, dissatisfaction, discontent; anger, rage, fury, wrath, indignation, resentment; embarrassment, mortification, humiliation, shame.
*New Oxford American Dictionary.

It's Lonely, in this place.
This place of heart ache, and pain.
Why do I choose to be here?
Do I feel heard? Do I want to?

Hear - be heard - Do I listen?

There was a rabbit who stopped by for
some tea, so the story goes...

Will we choose to feel soulful?
Does sorrow-full feeling gather energy
fight, holding us here till our doom;
empty rooms spinning anticipation,
of love coming home to stay:
MYSTERY...

Interest expanding horizon as we ignite
ourselves in life; curiosity calming
chaos, Loving each other, and in turn:
*Peaceful

*Peaceful - adjective
peaceful relations: harmonious, at peace, peaceable, on good terms, amicable, friendly, cordial, nonviolent.
*Wikipedia

**Feeling language, writing life. Drawn by courage
of survival...**

Why do I not believe? What holds me
back? Layers of bitterness thick in
unwilling heart. And so I distract
myself with habit...
...tidy in application,
chaotic in will.

Surviving, not thriving.

Equality from inside heart chambers,
dazzles mind with potential,
to feel happy sharing it with
others. Heart equal in acceptance
of another, distributing no dispute;
giving freely in love's desire
to honor peaceful intention;
thriving in love,
weaving heart's content.
(82)

In a sense,
time breaks and builds trust,
what we do with it.
Is that what it is?

As we move through new love, do we
begin to take advantage in sense of
habit - expecting other to behave in
particular manner. Do we accommodate
our response with anticipation of
assuming to know the thoughts of
another? Are we living in the future,
in our anticipation and so creating it
as we wait? Does one accept fully
other in capacity of being? Projection
not born of rejection, rather love
and so trust. Surrender. And what
do the moments we have build into?
Patience
Impatience
Kindness
Selfishness
Acceptance
Rejection
Surrender
Control
All combinations stating love, hatred.
Does love without condition exist?
In choosing we are born,
in choosing we may love, or hate.
In choosing what are we?
Calm/Agitated
Giving/Taking
Receiving/Projecting

Fair/Unequal
Does love without control exist?
Lifting in love soul purpose,
acquainted in equality.
In freedom, spirit aware.
Why does God know us and we of God?
Are we one in bond?
When we trust how we feel through our
hearts, our connection to God remains
open, to receive and give on God's
behalf - often what we know comforting
and blinding us from surrender.
(100)

I have felt extension of anger
in existence of feeling lonely,
not acknowledged - unable to connect
with myself, showing in critical
analysis of others. Do I push
responsibility away in desire to
possess? May I come to know trust,
learn to become it, cherish its
horizon, share myself with others
so that I may experience
sharing by way of its receipt,
responsive? And still, on the other
side of soulful being, wakes empty
heart with mind charge - anger
taking hold of slivers, the kind
that pierce the heart.
Truth in surfacing.
(125)

ANGUISHED EUPHORIA

Sometimes,
love sweeps eternal bliss
into our hearts,
long enough to taste it,
and long for more.

Sometimes,
blame wanders into
'that we keep close',
and concocts there.

Always,
God calls home to responsibility.

How do we get there?
Journey to God here on earth...

Remembering love?

...once Anguished Euphoric;
now heart's content...
(131)

So much of our existence based in that
which hurts our way, or so we may
perceive.

And choice requires energy.
Energy below the line

Energy above the line

The division of soul into black and
white, dark and light, evil and good.

All above and below the line of the
three hundred and sixty degrees
that we are.

One hundred and eighty degrees
- in which half do we choose
to linger longer?

And what is there to do
with what another has to say,
as it belongs to that self;
but reflection.
We create for ourselves.

And I imagine being sick is an
expression of love in lack.
Not because it is not given.

And in our non-receipt
do we blame our victim more?

Our vindication?
To love ourselves,
so that we may love others, and love
others, in order to know self.

In giving and receiving we balance
flow, as all alive must replenish.
While in life, linger longer.

(62)

Do we document our sadness.
Dare we document our joy.

Dare I document contribution,
that I may know to earn my keep.

And in trust?

We do not question
and we do not fear.

Feeling others happiness,
taking on their joy.

In sadness,
I learn from your sorrow.

and you lift mine with love.
Are we not?
Each other.
(105)

thinking out loud...

Nature of interaction where energy-motional heart lives in its moment of beating, representational of the cumulative moments of this, one particular being's existence - how can it be any other thing than a reflective process in which to learn about that which longs for healing within one's own emotions? I cannot claim voice for another. And yet sometimes I try to.

Energetic flow craves awareness of heart in those moments expressed in current. When I experience frustration, is it because I am unaware of the love my heart carries in those moments, being distracted by unconscious emotional reaction to an interaction? Emotional habit. Undoubtedly, emotional frustration is soul responsibility; duty of heart claims emotional ownership.

Energy of frustration offers gifts toward opportunity for release of negative energy held within being, of choice to become aware of frustration's intention for growth of soul and of the opening of heart further into love and acceptance. A question to ask is: How can I know another's emotional experience when I am physically particular to only my own? Am I? Physically particular to only my own?

We may sense what another feels and perhaps it is upon clarification, when mutual energetic flow is reached that an interaction becomes complete in its healing. It is easy for me to make assumptions based in fear of what others may think of me, and it is easy for me to turn my fear around and to apply its projection as a description of how another is being in an interaction - reading between the lines where imagination exists in quantum - and may it also become a goal to receive the gifts of reflection existing in interaction; gifts to be sure as they open mind to depths of heart expanding open communication, allowing acceptance to nurture equality.

Conscious Communication? Represents individual opportunity to participate responsibly within one's communicative contribution; emotionally, intellectually, verbally and physically. Perhaps conscious communication is owning one's own interpretation and perspective, along with subsequent reactions or responses toward relationship engagements, and is not about focusing on what 'the other person' involved in the relationship engagement is offering as a gauge for what one will offer in return to the interaction. Is it a process, of observing own reaction/response to what is being communicated, removing temptation to communicate anything that feels self serving and instead gaining clarification through acceptance and openness of being, holding emotions in such a way so as not to take another's communication personally; tuning in to what is needed to observe within self, striving to acknowledge highest good, to be gentle with the human element and that second chances are eternal for each regarding growth in communication.

I once told Ruby I thought that human interaction carries such subtle tones of negotiation that communication is easily consumed in competition without even realizing we are immersed in egos battle zone. That conflict is aroused when a person's silent, or obvious expectations are not met; expectation born of conditioning and selfish motivation that different people and environments come and go in our personal worlds, and within this framework, conscious communication is learning how to uphold and grow one's own personal vision and moral aptitude, while striving to understand, respect and include perspective of others in order to expand conscientiously, together. I would say to Ruby that I flounder.

What tangible form of creation does emotion evoke? What feeling in our body does a particular emotion denote? Feelings – a word we use to describe life force as it moves through one's being - evoke particular patterns of energy motions (e/motions) in the human body. E/motions lead us to our next 'move', the next physical action we take - based in how our intellect, by way of our mind, interprets the emotions, described through words we use to express our feelings resulting from the e/motion experienced. The e/motion we are feeling in this present moment represents result of all choices we have endeavored previous to now. While their cumulative effect is what

is now, we can trace back our steps to
gain understanding, and further use
this knowledge - based in experience -
to make different choices moving
forward, if desired. What action will
result of the current e/motional
feeling moving through your body now?
What will your next feeling be?
More of the same, or one of a different
tone? In paying attention to how we
feel when we are feeling an e/motion,
we empower ourselves to explore the
supreme nature of who we are in those
moments we experience fully. In paying
sincere intention toward a next
e/motion, we empower development of
trust in getting to know the physical
mechanics we nurture. Reflection is
a tool to be used for gaining clarity
and insight regarding e/motions we
experience. An act of reflection
exists within lapse of emotional
congruity, our being displaced from
being in the moment where the truth of
our nature exists for observation
through use of our senses as we are
experiencing them. Through reflection
we anticipate our intellect to
accurately describe that which has
already past, and to the extent that we
hold onto past energy patterns. A
moment before reflection is awareness
of e/motions being lived now - It is
speech without words; entering the

language of knowing. A timeless state
of breath flowing in currents unique to
each, while connected in essence of
All That Is, divine.
Digress, and expand.
Question it all.
(11)

Heart pure and true...the darker
side of humanness: I suppose, the
elements I experience in life which
pull me out of my flow, trap me
inside of myself where what I offer
is not of my truest nature,
exploring what lurks in the roots
of anger...
(116)

IMPATIENCE

A product of unfulfilled expectation
fostered by lack of willingness in
its moment to adjust to flow of
circumstance.
(89)

Within focused intention; perceptive
capacity, intuition, and imagination
build in expanse, encompassing that
which we have experienced; a
cumulation of advance in the pursuit
of love to the degree at which one
feels it; experiences it. The more
constant one feels being in a state
of love - opportunity being in both
giving and receiving of it - the
more joyful one feels, and becomes.
The more joyful one becomes, the
greater one's personal energy
vibration, becoming more and more in
tune with lightness of being,
eventually; one becomes all; all
become one, one by one succumbing to
the light we first departed from;
expanding infinity.

...imposition of social acceptance
reflecting oppositional atmosphere
to that of human nature.
(78)

DRINK IN DESIRE

I drink in your desire,
capturing hearts sweet knowing
that love is freedom
in your embrace.
(77)

❀

CHEMICAL LOVE
In a love state;
chemical love.
Language within language;
hypnotic euphoria:
euphoria anguished;
welcome peaceful wrath.

Energy changes as we do.
As thoughts impress
conscious awakening,
do we love?

Universe provides
upon meeting with patience;
Face of God beaming light
through eyes opening.
Chemically charged.
Universally bonded.
(130)
❀
❀

By placing our minds to follow
emotional reaction toward a present
moment,we solicit life prematurely in
the anticipating of future manifest
outcome. By emotionally reacting to
that which represents possibility of
projected outcome, though is not yet
formed in present; and is becoming
manifest as one's thoughts progress it,
we determine our energy motional
existence in realms of illusory
measure. By observation of energy now,
and following its flow with integrally
focused manifestation, one becomes
in natural flow - a truth full
representation of ones being. As our
minds race ahead, seeking unraveling of
future outcome, we rob ourselves of
nurturing within being now; feel what
you think, and become what you feel;
intention landing in manifest
atmosphere conducive to its purity.

(146)

lips of succulence, pounding of hearts
lightness of being, fresh love starts
shortness of breath, pulsing of time
moments of passion, new love finds
ebbing, probing, tongues of fire
hardness, dampness, smells desire

eternal
(156)

WAVES

Love not abiding sways long into night
surrendering to freedom's call.
Amongst sweat and longing
bodies crave heat
seeking penetrative ways.
Tempestuous bursting rocks heart waves
in binding fleshy desire.
Sensuous beings rocking in rhythm
to soul's intimate being.
Love burns doubtful mind.
Blessings found amidst turmoiled heart.
God calling our names in rapture.
Inviting us.
Love recognized in human capacity;
a gift meant to be shared;
honored in the partaking.
Witness to love found in bonding.
Expanding heart in mind of God.
Beauty abounding.
Love flourishing.

Waves of you inside of me.
(118)

So much for the afterglow. Unspeakable voices fill my head, unwilling to express depths of despair; our water suffocating in human greed upon yet another oil spill. And are we not guilty as we condemn our suppliers while basking in products for sale. And it's our WORLD FOR SALE. Petroleum most sought after natural resource, its greatness reduced to monetary value as we consume ourselves to death. WOW. Is this what we want? Really?

Water following suit. I wonder, who will buy and sell our air? And will we believe 'they' have a right to, and will we allow it as we do our energy, and now waters?

To feel love for another - what good does it do me pent up inside? Like a time bomb ready to go off and until we assume that we know what to do, we can not linger on from our hearts, our spirit out of balance while soulless in mind; heart knowing home of all. Does one choose to live without love? Is this why so few of us speak?

We scream from the bowels of voice in order to be heard - children understand and that is why we weep, young inside our birthright, unaware of nightmare to follow birthing; money, and those who crave it above all, and in the taking ungrateful in selfish gain, mass market their intentions.

What about word of mouth? Let the world and all in it, you, me, choose for ourselves whether we as connected beings and what we offer are worthy of each other, and in our expectation, become it; worthy. Expanding as far as word of mouth grows it.

QUIT INVADING MY LIFE. No one should be forced to live a lifestyle that serves so very few. So many of us recipients of fallout from greed.

And what about you? What would you share of your heart, that you have not dared to speak? What do you? Are we meant to, share that which evokes magnanimous love inside, massaging our souls with emotional cooperation; our dance with life. Is it a brawl? A festival?

Heart and mind are one. As every living 'thing' is partner with its own extreme; mild to intolerant, we scale our time in love's embrace not knowing we are already there - we search for it, in as many different ways there are of our world. All Billions of us. We each have a role to play. The 'destitute' and the 'riches'. There is have and have not in mind delusion. Can we set ourselves free? Do we understand how? Do we want to?

Those who feel fight with great anticipation, inviting balance to settle amongst chaos offer one half of our equation. The other accepting without condemnation all encompass both. There is no enemy except for the one who fights. The other side feels what we feel in their own interpretation of circumstance.

And as I sit here writing on my laptop computer, I cannot help but feel catastrophe amongst beauty.

Do you feel powerless? At times I do, and yet know we are not. Not when we work alongside another. Each of us caring solely for one other - approximately 3 and a half billion partners. Communing without labels...

What do we make our commitments to?

An offering of bread? Water?

STRINGS OF THOUGHT

There is music in my head, bouncing
off drums inside my ears. And as
the dog pouts, the cat works her way
into the pack. I am hungry, there
has been no time to rest, I am
tired. Exhausted? Time to heal.
Wounds feel large, and in their
stature I succumb. Not quite sure
to what. It's dark, and heavy, and
it wrestles with my mind. Permeates
my body with intention born other to
soul. Mind status. There seems a
quicker way to sleep than to knock
self to knees in defeatist despair.
Challenges many along this road
travelled, sinkage until we aim no
higher. Treadmills of heart
abandoned for quick version - lust
full. Are we intertwined, beyond
connected vision? Our ancestors and
theirs communicating vibrations of
sound - learning how to be with
human body. In knowledge we
progress - at times beyond heart,
relying solely with sense of mind,
other senses unattained in prognosis
- feelings of imbalance? Strings of
thought; emotional wave lengths in
tune to energy motional being?
(128)

Anguished euphoric: body action.
Anguished euphoria: peaceful in wrath.
Balanced euphoric: content in mind.
Do we receive and choose emotional
reaction expressed through our bodies
connection with surroundings; life.
All parts of it. Nothing dead;
sleeping in its shadow. Dwelling in
heart's discontent?
And then, do we love who we are or
roast our imperfections instead of
feeding them life, to become accepted
in acceptance. To rework hatred in to
some form of manageable rage, agree to
disagree - choosing that which makes us
happy, respecting that which anger
longs for - acknowledgement. Can we
love, without being sexual? We are
sexual beings, light beings, emotional
beings; connected beings.
Commitment, is curious passtime;
curious hobby. A leisurely roll through
passage of time, rocking our ships in
cold water - body temperature
emotionally cold, even while warmed
by life source.
We are born to love.
To be peacefull in our wrath.
Loving, alongside sex.
Humble, alongside war.
Receiving in the giving.
Perception is what is.
In what do we thrust?

Truly great departing weak
and trembled soul.
(164)

I recognize within emotions,
fear of success, disguised as lack
in belief of ability to act towards
achievement of goals; manifesting
inaction, creates failure before
opportunity to act of inspired
thought. How does one shift from
paralysis state of being; that which
is in-between mind ability to think
and bodies ability to act upon
thought, into action determining
divine purpose?   Holding belief,
and faith, requires action born of
intuition in realizing dreams to
fruition. Reserving belief and
faith, naked of action, creates
atmosphere in energy of waiting on
life to find its way toward one's
being; building stagnation.

Beyond paralysis: applying intuitive
mindset to action propels energy
forward, nurturing respect, building
trust, growing ability in order one
may shine through light within
being; acknowledging
Divinity in all.
(40)

Are feelings intellectual response
to emotional reactions
born of sensory stimulus?

In a world seen as 360 degrees
do we judge or observe?

Judgement:
subjective determination; intellect
driven affecting emotional state;
indicates ability to choose
state of being.

Observation:
sensory driven,
no effect on itself,
being driving force;
indicates inability to choose;
experiencing energy as is.

Choice leads ability
to observe energy as is,
or,
to judge;
fabricate
in search of tangible meaning
to express spiritual experience?
(176)

I have placed value on owned energy,
the kind we claim to do, be, know;
thinking removed from energy of what
is going on now, while choosing to
copy action of past, and thinking
ahead of time to who we are in order
to exist in present. Avoiding truth
in flow. Energy twists while
bringing past into future,
and future into past; eliminating
choice. We are time travelers,
whether travelled in day or in
night. And do we steal our futures
while we dance in love of plight?
(158)

Whether intimate or passerby,
we touch each other.
Energy binding our souls.
Feeding ourselves with dreams
and nightmares.
Mind allowing the body to age
through misinterpretation
and misdirected communication.
(117)

BIRTHING

A glance at the clock suggests she go
back to sleep, to awaken her mind
to all that would willingly come
in preparation for snow to fall;
a blanket of love covering indiscretion
from previous season, where all that
was dreamt of faded yet into fantasy.

And as it goes with each new season,
death, and birth be-stills us; and the
fly stumbles upon its back amidst the
changing season, as does mind in
slumber; and rebirth awaits our eyes to
welcome opportunity upon our lids
awakening. Will the day be rewarded
with trespass, or participation?

And as mind embarks in the dawning;
emotion grants movement to those who
feel, and heed the call; a resolve of
surrender to the rhythm of one's heart,
to the beat of mind, to one's breath in
tune with Nature; while amid and beyond
shadows of death; birthing,
life precedes all.

(32)

EXPECTANCY DELAYS

Human malfunction.
Love truly is the greatest teacher.
Lead in love's expectation.
(111)

STATURE

breath; motion = movement;
directed by spirit,
guided by mind,
transmitted through brain
to body via nervous impulse.

What makes one pulse?

How do we live?

How do we receive each other?

I you...

Do stars whisper
amongst themselves...

Sharing Shine
(157)

❀

GRACE

An act of Grace,
seeks as high a noble standing
as one's heart may sustain,
placing value of another's heart
equal to and greater than one's own.
Within admission;
an act of Grace holds selflessness
at core of creation
in order that love may flourish;
grace full being bearing witness
to the reflection of joy
in soul of ONE.

(45)

❀

Genius: Vision of heart in action?

Aren't we all, Genius?

Potential at home in passion...

WHISPERING LOVE'S INTENTION

This morning I woke
to light nudging soul;
tempting my heart in song.

Images felt.

Love without fear
as none in the giving.
Guilt not abiding.

Freedom bound in physicality.
Love flourishing transcendence.

This morning I tasted cruelty;
absent of malice,
wicked in love's longing.

Desire intertwined;
fragile in strength,
strengthened, by fragility.

Believed. Trusted. All Knowing.

Denial treads softly, lurking.
Bringing us to our knees
in humbled gratitude
...whispering love's intention.

(106)

What about anger? Do we let them pass? Moments of anger, selfish intentions. Do they add to the definition of who we are? Each time I feel angry I feel disservice to the Universe, God, Spirit. And just like God we have a name, an essence. Is God's essence, Spirit, the breath we breathe, the connections we maneuver our lives through? We are recognition. And how long will I hold anger? Until I die amidst its grave?...perhaps.

Please, zap me out of my narrow mindset, I'd much rather spend time with you. My earth family begins while in the womb, extended to those in contact with. Did I pass you by? Have I seen your smile? Did I look you in the eye and know, that you saw my heart, felt my soul. Did you offer yours?

Did I avert? Did I avoid? Did I look away in hopes of disconnect? In disconnect do I advocate myself and deny you? And then do I treat another with varying degrees of distain? Do I disrespect and dichotomize? So many questions...

Am I Bipartite? And if I am then aren't we all? And am I not then all of you, and you, me? One relationship at a time, one with life. LOVE, that transcends all. Will you receive me - when I love you? Will you give your heart in order I may try?

Tasting Love - Dare we? In tasting love we must also be it as we are what we consume. Love is Medicine. Let it Be. Body knows, mind interprets.

In mistrust do we loose perspective?
Of what is true? Does one become
negative in energy offered as a way of
defense, deflecting hurt full emotions?
And when we are feeling hurt, do we
close our hearts to receiving? When we
feel unhappy, do we retain negative
emotion in favor of feeling rejection,
bypassing our soul's intention? Afraid
of processing emotion that cause
physical pain in the body. Are we a
sick humanity because of choice to
ignore that we have complete and total
power to be the best that we can
possibly be, that, in fact, it is our
duty to one another to try: to release
our bonds of misery so that both and
all may become free. To exist - no
boundaries but for what is contained in
freedom. Anger dissolves in happiness.
It is possible for all of humanity to
experience peaceful being. To
encompass each other with warmth,
caring, co-existing. One step at a
time. There is enjoyment to be held
in kindred spirit. We are responsible
for every living soul, for every form
of life if we want to preserve our own:
what do we give back in gratitude for
our consciousness?
Please, God, if we don't have the
option to try, take me now from this
torture chamber.
(122)

Within sadness, pure joy lends
itself in greatest abandon, for when
we are low joy must endeavor itself
equal to and greater than the loss
of itself.

A vast journey it is;
becoming one's joy in existence.
In sadness, beauty beckons to be
nurtured and received; to feel
accepted. And when denied do we
shrink within influence of
opposition?

Beauties plight in life is but to
exist - we are receptors,
as we also gift in return.
Joy and love synonymous.

When we lose site of joy, when we
replace it with vibrationally lower
emotion of itself, joy becomes lost
in hearts confusion; indecision
filling part of whole. Within
indecision, feelings of lack
consume lead; mind follows suit.
Around in circles we go.

The beauty of beauty,
is in its ability to weather mind's
torment - beauty shines, spiraling
upward in natural flow,
we need only seek its rays.
(51)

Get real? Temptation taking hold
of imaginary salutation in pursuit
of who I am now, conscientiously
distracted. And in silence do we
    honor commitment to plight of
destruction, blaming each other
until we bleed ourselves dry of
resources, life force shamed in our
presence, consumed by our choices.

Go ahead, deny IT.

Love IT change our light.
(126)

HARMONIES CALL

When culture reflects harmony with
Nature the world will know peace.
(52)

PERMISSION TO FREEDOM

In permission
we are expectation free,
having given permission to freedom;
in freedom we are bound by concept;
in trust we open to possibility.
(155)

I was thinking, I can take the
language I speak in my mind and
learn to know how my body feels as I
am speaking in my thoughts. What do
I feel as I say something or take
action toward something? Is it a
loving or unloving feeling? If I
want to remove the feelings that are
undesirable to me, then I can
replace them with the feelings I do
want to feel, freely growing in the
experience of joy propelled by
desiring more of that which drives
my heart. When I remain emotionally
attached to imagining only about
removing what I don't want and will
no action to make it happen, then I
will remain in limbo until my
body-mind and soul are in harmony
with life force; growing radiance.

(145)

Caressed of water's silken touch,
nibbled by warmth;
heat saturates
cavity expanding to life;
love tempts reveal;
rejuvenation of cells
through inhalation of Spring,
breathing Peace.

(140)

Living in a state of denial is the
act of desiring something other than
what we are currently creating in
each moment, and, not partaking in
conscious acts to change the moments
in our lives to represent our
personal truth. In holding awareness
of our heart's desire in each
current moment, we allow our life
creations to become co-creative, by
way of spirit moving through us,
transforming the energy resulting
from experiences of denial; human
'dilemmas', to the receiving of the
gift of divine flow into our lives,
naturally resulting in the
transference of love from our 'own'
hearts to others.
(28)

LOVE CAME ROUND TO FIND ME.
It's not about the background, it is
3D version, right here, right now
and next relation. Love tends to the
broken hearted, often silent, al-
ways true. Gentled spirit moved my
soul and love came round to find me,
it bound me to her. A golden an-
gel. Soon I will take flight.
(143)

RESIDENT MOTION
I was mean, whether direct,
or indirectly: I am angry.
Internal rage silent in application.
Coverage smile to protect that which
hurts too much to let go, a painful
memory: life, and love; cheated.
Learning to love all
that we share surroundings with
letting go of anger, choosing
to believe in something different.
Gain new perspective holding truest in
heart, intellect not compromised.
And is it true? We are here,
to learn to love: coexist peacefully.
To choose it in order to help it grow
- neither exuberance nor shyness,
in balance of energetic equality.
'Being in the moment' A term overused?
Where equal in emotion creates
attention; focus, remembering;
distraction-less.
If we were truly in the moment
would time then not exist?
Without distraction, energy balanced:
do we become resident motion?
Equal in opportunity
amongst believers in heart.
Our intentions common,
spirit creatively flourished;
unique per human code.
Are we without conscience to the degree
we are not fully awake in our dream?
(173)

NOT GUILTY; PEACE FULL WRATH

In ***desolation** do we fill our hearts
with ***greed**? Binding ourself to the
nighttime adventure. Stoney in our
heart's content, we slay. And in
madness we live, tempted by shallows
heart. And Not Guilty; Peace full in
wrath. What do you love? Will you?
Love? My fear is great and so my
insanity grows larger than life living
outside of myself. Shots fired not
worth the blow. Do I tempt? ***Cajole**?
Am I ***witness**. Emerging...
Why do we do what we do?
(30)

*desolation |ˌdesəˈlā sh ən| (noun)
a state of complete emptiness or destruction
anguished misery or loneliness

*greedy|ˈgrēdē|
adjective (greedier , greediest)
having or showing an intense and selfish desire for
something, esp. wealth or power : greedy thieves who
plundered a defense contractor.
• having an excessive desire or appetite for food

*cajole |kəˈjōl| (verb)
persuade someone to do something
by sustained coaxing or flattery

*witness |ˈwitnis| (verb)
1 have knowledge of (an event or change)
from personal observation or experience

*THE RIGHT WORD

The desire for money and the things it can buy is often associated with Americans. But not all Americans are greedy, which implies an insatiable desire to possess or acquire something, beyond what one needs or deserves (:greedy for profits). Greedy is especially derogatory when the object of longing is itself evil or when it cannot be possessed without harm to oneself or others (: a reporter greedy for information). Someone who is greedy for food might be called gluttonous, which emphasizes consumption as well as desire (a gluttonous appetite for sweets). A greedy child may grow up to be an avaricious adult, which implies a fanatical greediness for money or other valuables. Rapacious is an even stronger term, with an emphasis on taking things by force (so rapacious in his desire for land that he forced dozens of families from their homes. Acquisitive, on the other hand, is a more neutral word suggesting a willingness to exert effort in acquiring things (: an acquisitive woman who filled her house with antiques and artwork), and not necessarily material things (a probing, acquisitive mind). Covetous, in contrast to acquisitive, implies an intense desire for something as opposed to the act of acquiring or possessing it.
*New Oxford American Dictionary

Do we provide ourselves with guilt
around preconceived notions   that
something we have said, done or thought
about may elicit a negative,
unsupportive or judgmental reaction
from others? Every interaction lives
from moment to moment - judgment an
illusion we project and receive whether
we are 'judging' ourselves, 'judging'
others or fearing the judgment of
others while caught in the projection
of our own denial. Other than getting
caught in the illusion the idea of
judgment creates, study the
exponential nature of thought and the
path those thoughts travelled upon
becoming realized. Upon reaching full
understanding of one's thoughts and the
organization, or sequential order of
them, how thoughts flow into one
another to the point where they are
brought to life; we will have been
touched with opportunity to realize an
experience of truth within that
instance. There is no judgment in truth
- there is being in truth. When we
judge, we live within fear of
separateness, projecting action
resulting of emotions created of that
fear, a fear we intuitively know is
unwarranted as we are all connected by
way of our higher being; spirit, and
that we truly are never alone.
Resulting of our action motivated

through fear, we further engage in
action of illusion of judgment,
creating negative energy towards others
and ourselves. Judgment's ultimate
power represents itself in WAR. The
releasing of manifestation of judgment
is but a thought process away...
(6)

❀
❀
❀ ❀
❀ ❀ ❀

"Believe nothing,
no matter where you read it,
or who said it, no matter if I have said it,
unless it agrees with your own reason
and your own common sense".
~ B u d d h a ~

❀ ❀ ❀
❀ ❀
❀
❀

To Mother Earth...

Building anxiety threatens my sanity;
emotional outlets wanted.

Are people gathering?
To partake silent action?
Heart Grown.

Mother Earth,
I AM SORRY

I have squandered, pillaged,
held regard for money as high priority.

Room for Love?

For there is no money inside of heart;
Money does not make heart grow.

May we hear highest bidders?
Agenda slammed into our throats
until we swallow and become;
image.

I AM SORRY

Life minds blind to the living,
our devastation paving way.

For how many more lives
will be lost to the lining
of another human's pockets?

HOW MANY SUFFERINGS?

Condemned Sacrifice.
How do we feel center,
when pursuit of oil consumes our lead,
greed in our ambition...

...sucking soul from within,
subliminal in tendency;
master of deeds directing.

How many times more
will we fall victim?
At least as many as I do.

I AM SORRY
...I did this.
HELP US

Show us what to do.
Dare I ask for mercy.
Will mercy GATHER.
And LOVE gives us strength
to act on behalf of other;

MOTHER EARTH
longing to connect.
We may not be early,
are we too late?

OUR HISTORY
Gather & Grow.
PEACEFUL in WRATH
(31)

In ways that soul manifestation holds
energy in its living organism, poses
who/what we are in matter. Energy and
mass are of the same while mass is
condensed form of energy, or, anything
forming more than pure energy is energy
condensed. The speed of light must
contain within it density; mass in
varied form of matter, or light would
not exist, nor be seen or measurable -
the more dense in form, the less light
lives there, yet still being of it.
Pure light is blinding to spirit's
optical receptors - as is the absence
of light blinding - as vibration of
pure light is in excess of recognition
for that of the physical body; less
intensified light experienced implies
of soul's existence;
of that which moves
within human physical vibration; matter
more condensed, the light not easily
penetrating nor in human being easily
absorbed, and all the while tantalizing
through demonstration of existence
outside of darkness recognition of the
light in one's being. Opening mind to
physical energy motions (emotions)
expands knowledge of soul; light being.
Perhaps light is energies first
manifestation. Perhaps we fear the
dark in our denial of it being a part
of our essence. In some ways,
traditional religion persecutes Nature,

inability to understand, or
unwillingness to see, thwarted in
perception that humans must thrive to
become wholly good. Misunderstood
darkness becoming enemy to light, which
all the while they are one,
each other in varying degree.
(165)

Within vulnerability toward energy-
motion we refer to as love, runs equal
in momentum personal power which exists
and demonstrates its expanse in ability
of peace full being. An expansion of
heart wraps and weaves its memory by
and through balance of intellectual
thought and physical energy-motion;
transposition of experience showing in
tangible form that we are, and in the
moments we become. Spiritual growth
and physical healing; practicality in
thought combined with awareness of
emotive being.

Vision entails focus of direction,
its progress being lost to what is
occurring now, as validation of one's
success of purpose beholds selflessness
in all form. Soul fulfillment requiring
freedom from knowing - allowing faith
to carry us toward our destiny; purpose
fulfilled in direction toward higher
purpose, regardless of where it lands
in this life. Forward motion is
timeless; measure of progress lives in
duality as seducement of linear mind.
Purpose evolves while tangible being
accesses depths of being propelled
in faith, propagating love.

In selflessness, love is gifted toward
expansion of all hearts combined,
raising soul vibration and evolution of
mind, infinity being that which human
mind has not yet perceived, and strives
toward. Destination unfolds in Being,
knowing all that is necessary in
support of forward energy-motion of
one's purpose now.

In waking of soul,
competition becomes nurtured by love,
giving way to propagation of life
force. Equality in Being discovered in
Unity, where feet STAND.
(41)

PEACEFUL INTENTION

the world continues
in atmosphere divided
between extremes emanating from core
where nature of who we are
encompass and distributes
experience and perception
from one conception
perception is born
from there compilation of thought
and thought cumulation
guiding where we stand
as a whole, now
if peace is desired be peaceful
for to badger soul of another
is to badger oneself
in the action
action represents
and who we are...
representing rates
at which thought
and emotion create
together in unison
thought guided by spirit
bodies transmit
through its nervous system
vibration of soul
moving through
brain translating
all that we are
heart making sense
of non sense
(91)

MERCY

humble embrace
expansion of love sets us free
understood
silent rage alongside asylum keeper
grants immunity
from holding pits of pain
blinding vision
static electricity
running through our veins
hyped on synthetic
crying
starving
killing each other
and above all
to hold god within full vision;
flow of mercy

(46)

About God?

In mind's weakness one's will must flourish, or perish.

And must it be that we are less than human in our ways? Preposterous in notion that we may live freely, unduly harmed in love and hardship.

Honor, integrity, loyalty. Who sets the terms? How do we abide? Where does our direction come from? Is it from our own free will? Is it will of God? Is it just what is and then what it becomes. And all that we name God belongs not to ourselves as we feign responsibility?

Do we replace God with government; those we may disagree with, and yet follow? Do we feel disconnected, and so fight to our deaths in our quest to know what is real. In the name of truth, we fight and perish.

And for what? For some, material gain over and above health and well being of all else on the planet. We all know each other, can we bare to look, dare we care?

Dare we stop the insanity? Will you? Love so deeply it scares you into denial of existence. Will I?

Are we meant to find that one true mate, one who sees truth in way that adds to our own - we give, as sown in return. Animal beings do not falter within acceptance, fault born in perspective.

I believe one of the greatest gifts we experience in being human is trusting in something greater than ourselves. It is where hope lives, and sanity dwells. It is where lack of faith may be nurtured in loss of itself, where bounty of kindness lives longing to be partaken, in order it may be shared.

When I feel doubt full, I call on that which is greater than my ability to connect is in those moments of doubt, traveling inward to promote outward expression. I trust this place of expansion, of what spawns heart. God speaks in as many ways as there are spirits unified in soul. Magnanimous in being as it encompasses the bits and pieces of all that we are. Unity; desired connection, acceptance in shared interaction.

In connection, dare I spend time with it? Get to know what I am feeling? How it attributes to my daily action, my choices. Is there something so great to fear? Perhaps you won't accept me for who I am? All while I want you to accept me when I haven't yet accepted myself, nor taken full responsibility for all action on my behalf.

I visit sadness, energetic pain in these moments of self-rejection. And how long do we hold them for? Our moments of self-rejection? For as long as we hold anger we deny ourselves opportunity to thrive in light nature. To be lifted in the Grace of One.

At times Grace feels an impossibility, its elegance born of pure intention.

As we wind our way, soul connected in search of awareness of the joy in the mystery life represents, we are cherished, extraneous beings; are we tired?

There is nothing quite like caring for another's spirit to energize the soul. Helping is growing in nurturing self. Feeling who we are in order what we give comes from place of clarity, balanced energy; body felt and acknowledged by our thoughts, creating what becomes our daily life.

Tired? Wake up...I said to myself - WAKE UP!

And I thought, what is the emotion behind the image? The heart behind, and before mind. What if I were to choose. Choose to remember that it is through our hearts that we are born, and reproduce. That mind takes over - its temptation greater than ability to choose moderation. What if I were to take what I need, and then give more - creating abundance.

Replenish Natural Harmonization.

What if? I asked myself...

What if I were to honor highest good?

What if I were to believe in love?

What if I were to respect Nature?

Ruby would often say of Nature, that the heart of a ruby red apple grows from the inside out, its core expanding until its perish, and still, right then, is alive in other form; a material succumbing; a cumulative spiritual birth. The life last consciously led dissolved to earth in order that spirit may once again fly. In truth, full; completion.

I think back to my story and remember, all that time I spent receiving anger, receiving rage.

And for what purpose?

I remember the day I chose to leave. My abuser had told me he wanted to drive back to the doctor we had seen the past weekend. There was no reason for it, we had no appointment. I knew from the deepest place in my heart that he wanted to finish what he hadn't the first time around. I knew I would not get a second chance - that I would be dead that beautiful Autumn day.

I was driving to the bank, and once I got back we would leave for the drive to my death.

He said to me, "I want you back by 2:00pm so we can drive to the doctor's office. You are coming back..." I looked at my cat, and my dogs. I looked around the room and then I looked at him and with reassurance told him yes, I'm coming back. I looked at the clock and saw it was 1:00pm, and considering it would take me two hours to drive to the bank and back again, I felt his set up for revenge. I walked into our bedroom and scanned, until my sights landed on one possession that was precious to me.

As I drove away, feeling stunned by apprehension, with my ID and the clothes on my back, and a necklace in my pocket my girlfriend had made me I started to sob. And between my sobs I begged, and I pleaded with God to keep me safe. I promised that if God helped me just one more time, that I would do my part, whatever my part may be. In my appeal I lost all sense of myself.

As I drove away, I felt a shift deep within my core. I did not yet realize I was leaving. As I drove, anxiety and panic fueled my energy. Soon I was racing at 120mph - frantic. As I continued to plead with God for mercy, I became aware, my actions were leading my desire to escape. Feeling devastation in my realization that I was leaving my animal companions, waves of grief surrounded me. I sobbed in resignation.

The animals in my life had become my source of inspiration, and comfort. Often consoling me into the wee hours of the night, we would curl up together, huddling, frightened, trusting each other. The thought of leaving them with him wounded my heart, played havoc with emotion running through.

After my escape, each night I wrote in a journal. Each night, I would list every emotion I remembered experiencing during the day and would expand on those emotions individually. Friends helping me out ensured that I promise to not contact my abuser. At first, I was able to promise for a few hours at a time, as guilt and fear clung me to my torment and so my facilitator, my tormentor.

Eventually, a few hours turned into a half a day, which turned into one day, two days, one week, two weeks - until I was strong enough to take full responsibility for choices that created safety and well-being for my spiritual and physical life.

I think back and remember the hatred and deceit. The manipulation and control. The wishing it would change, and believing he would. How each time the beatings would get worse, and each time I would make more room for the violence to continue by adapting myself to the pain.

What prompted me to leave? What saved my life?

It was a combination of feeling desperation and remembering. Remembering how I felt when emotion landed upon my mother's face and waves of sadness enveloped me in the knowledge that the next time she saw me it would be in my death - I did not want this for her. The emotion so overwhelmed me, she gave me strength, her spirit pure with love. In those moments I decided though my tormentor was taking my life, that if I was going to die, I was going to die with a smile on my face, that he could not take away what belonged to me in truth, an inherent ability to choose how I wanted to feel. In those last moments, my mother's strength gave me courage to quit fighting. I chose peace. I lifted the corners of my mouth until I felt my body smile, and I surrendered, accepted my plight and fully let go of my physical body. My arms limped to stillness as my body relaxed in the bliss my mind endeavored.

I died.

And then I was reborn. As spirit left my flesh, consciousness fading into energy, supported in physical death, my body gasped for air. As I choked and sputtered and regained awareness into my body, my abuser fully released his clutch. Several moments passed in this exchange. Not to be outdone he opened the door, threw my body out of the car onto the ground and proceeded to stand overtop of me dripping with sweat, screaming obscenities, kicking, punching, controlling. Once more his hands groped for my throat. As he wrapped his fingers around my neck I lifted my leg to his crotch. In his fits of rage, I did not fight back, I did not want to feel what he felt in the beatings. For they were tainted with hatred and they belonged to him. Somehow, when I deliberately raised my foot to his crotch and stopped with just enough pressure to let him know I could if I wanted to, he released, peeled himself off of me, and said "I've had enough, get in the car we're going home."

Silence welcomed me there.

As we drove in silence, I felt dumfounded. His expectation that life would go on as 'normal' no longer held my heart - it had been replaced with great sorrow, the kind a human feels when grieving the loss of a loved one. I was letting go.

Emotionally, my escape was not easy. I had reached a place where I knew with every cell of my being, my physical life would end if I chose to stay. One week after being strangled, and after four years of abuse at the hands of my tormentor, I found courage enough to save my life, having chose it.

Ruby was with me every step of the way, inside of my soul, cheering for me, allowing me to find my way. As did my mother's heart.

```
          a gift of time
          a lift of heart
           about Mercy?
          Mercy is full
          with intention
      the kind that lifts the heart
   it cannot exist without forgiveness
        and implied heartache
          mercy redeems
           within Mercy
      there is much to be thankful
             for ...
          heart propels
          as love swells
            merciful
           breathing...
          peaceful tide
             (180)
```

All this time I have been searching
for something that doesn't exist.
Who I am. All this time who I am is
what I do each moment I choose to
live; forgotten in moments I aspire
toward an image I hold to validate
my being. And what is it that I am
but how I feel? What I see in you,
the world surrounding, is how I
choose to be in its action of
living; expressing ourselves. And in
love I long to be, to become, to
giveaway; freedom lives here.
(86)

Imagine,
energy waves float along side each
other, creating friction when two or
more energies collide to make it so.
Impact between energies displaced
through human action,
and interaction - world in action at
once - born of thought;
being energy strands combined;
communal thought creation.
(34)

CHANGE ME

Change weakness in soul
into greater character of being.

Change me
when I cannot know love
for one but another.

Let me love all
within and through heart,
my heart within all I am.

Lift me up
that I may be humbled
in your presence;
Divinely Inspired.
Collectively Conscious.
Individually Whole.

Destined
to give and receive;
Love
Compassion
Empathy

Peaceful in Strength.

Change weakness in mind
toward greater awareness of character.

Change me
when I cannot know myself
and blame another.

And let me love all
within and through heart,
my heart within all I am.

Lift me up,
that I may lift others
and be lifted
by those inspired there.

Helping each other.

Humanely Unified and Identified.

Change strength I learn
into greater understanding;
life force greatest in highest good.

And when I see darkness,
Change me into light.

That it may shine between us.

Love Copious.
(115)

Perhaps other people will see me,
and like me. I've grown physically
tired from facade. Weary. Longing
to break through skin, to exist in
harmony, break free of existence
within visually, audibly,
sensory deprivation.

Affection robbed by own tenacity.

Senses create world we experience.
How we see color, taste nourishment,
smell air, hear nature, touch.
How we experience and express
in relation to our environment
is perspective.

What is your perspective? I cannot
know another's world as I am not
another's senses, and none can know
mine but myself. Understanding
grows in silence, at times unseen,
always appropriate. And do we claim
to know another before we know self?

In knowing this self I become one;
with spirit of mind in unit, body to
interpret energy, moving equal in
pace with mind's observation, delayed
through physical, mental emotional
and spiritual malnutrition.

Within ourselves grows outward
expression, that which we share with
our world; our families, friends,
relatives of relatives. Life.

And while participating in outward
expression, in shyness I recognize
humbled opportunity, and at times,
growth of disrespect thwarts
energies needed flow; choosing no
acceptance through action of
judgment; superior in criticism of
others, inferior in chastising of
self. Rejection. Stagnation. In
shyness, love breathes shallow
breaths, longing to express.
Acknowledgement.

All Human. All Animal. All Mammal.
All Plant. All Life. Each human,
expressing bits of soul in Unison.
Father, Brother, Sister, Mother,
Other, Me, and as so, You.

Bits of myself I claim in wake of
your smile. Translucent beauty
- triathlete of human spirit.
Bring me home.
(68)

Is it relative, what of one's past
is friend to confusion
and unawareness in current tense?
Is one richer for the experience of
recognizing what one feels now,
of one's nurturing ability to change
that which does not flow?
Are benefits forthcoming of
revisiting past influence or of
hyper planning the future when what
is going on is now, in this moment?
Is there balance between past and
future; a carrying of wisdom
forward; an accumulation of
experience landing the heals of
presence while affording intuition
opportunity to visit its
manifestations?
Does synchronistic regard of one's
journey past and future;a respectful
awareness of the cumulative nature
of emotional experience that we have
come to be, alongside that which
comes of intuition; a holding space
of open mind for intuitive guidance
to find its way to human action,
land in realm of personal truth in
present tense? And does successful
combination of All That Is balance
flow of ones personal truth of now,
affording peaceful experience of
being?
Reaching Middle Ground
(29)

KINDLE SOUL

Kindle my soul
bring me home.
Awaken in me
stones I throw;
learning.

Kindle my soul
bring me home.
Trust in heart
what I am shown;
believing.

Kindle my soul
bring me home.
Holding up love
no longer alone;
Standing.

Kindle Soul
(67)

GRAVITY

Is gravity god and god gravity? Is
gravity timeless because its motion
is constant? As we participate in
forward motion, time accumulates;
timeless in space where tuned
with gravity; Energy merging God?
(124)

**WHY DO HUMANS COUNT TIME? I WONDER WHAT
WOULD HAPPEN IF 'THE WORLD' STOPPED COUNTING?**

THOUGHTS?

Why do humans
think without control?
Are thoughts life force?
Will one die
without generating new ones,
not contributing to growth and
expansion? Does gravity hold us
connected to the earth, or does our
breath; gravity description of human
weight compared to buoyancy of air
in a human body. Is a floating log
to water as a human body is to the
earth, supported in force greater
than itself? Is brain to human as
spirit is to mind; life force
compelled in being?
(139)

Soulful song harmonic vibration of
voice quivers belly of
being, expressing
from deep within e-motion. When
shallow upon spirit reflection, not yet
learned to give love and receive in
return - laced with lust? Abandoned
for guilty pleasure? Food? Drink?
Complacent agreement? In love do we
moderate our desire to
honor, to acknowledge
and pledge its return? Do we
believe? Like minds together, ensuring
success for those of our kind?

A Human Race; Infinitely connected and
spiritually directed. Awareness of
our future needed now.
There is something
to be done, that we each can do:
participate in love's reciprocation.
Why wait? Tomorrow truly does not come
in its non-existent state, but
for in our minds. Now is the
'time'. Gather. Peaceful
in tension's intention.
(103)

Craved validation in hope of boosted
self confidence: this form of acceptance
sought, due lack of believing fully
in self? Skimming surface of trust.
Building self-confidence through
acceptance of heart and truths it
longs to express. No one else can
provide, journey being inward. Life
process: learning energy of trust upon
choosing it. Deciphering successful
attempts, and building from there.
(167)

Conscious choice requires that each
choice, for each moment, is made with
focused intention/attention; removing
tendency to create one's life through
habitual reaction. Habitual modes of
behavior 'kick' in when we neglect to
turn our thinking brain with conscious
mind on, in accordance with emotions
moving through our being. By allowing
our habitual mind to dictate our lives,
we miss a step in the filtering process
that is required for messages from our
higher being to reach our human level
of understanding while still somewhat
intact regarding the truth full intent
behind messages gifted by spirit. How
do we bridge the gap between our

Anguished. I feel as though, I may
not ever come back up from the
sadness I feel in the depths of my
hatred. I cannot breathe fully
here. And so I suffocate my body,
slowly, aging it to core; stimulant
replacing exercise to feel whole.
'Adulteress' pleasure holds captive
inside my head, and so in body. And
we all rage and plunder - with
smiles on our faces. Ignoring our
truth in heart. Our judgement
feeding anger until we forget who we
are in loves honor. Until the world
knows peaceful living, we'll consume
in our greed and turn a blind eye
to catastrophic nature. Caring from
distance great enough to not have to
feel, action it; care in vain,
intention blemished as not
recognized in movement, needed once
more in home of recognition.
Starving. We are responsible.
Money greater than God's will.
Abundance reap and squander.
Anguished in perish, turmoiled in
choice. Yet there is symmetry in
chaos, serving silence;
Anguished Euphoria:Peaceful Wrath
(33)

To love without fear is to tempt po-
tential's peak, in order it may grow;
rebirth. Trust requires action, for
if no step is ventured, blindness of
heart blackens one's soul, as sure
as light darkens. Opportunity born
in the dawn. In fear frustration ex-
poses self-imposed limits, where un-
fulfilled expectation lifts blame to
defense; fooling no one, condemning
all. In reaching for potential, honor
fully, love the greatest offering.
(70)

Containment: An imagined perimeter
of energy that in its totality is
greater than what inward it
contains. Itself being newest
addition to the growth of the whole;
and within containment one comes to
experience freedom, an understanding
of how life feels in its absence
- belief entertained -
an understanding into depths of
loss, love secure in roots.
All of it beautiful.
(64)

One may move through a process of
'letting go' within identifying one's
own subjective manifestations. In
paying attention to energy patterns
specific to our particular being
(feelings and physical emotions
surrounding an experience in any
current moment?) one creates an
environment for personal
observation, with possibility of
owning a balanced perception of our
personal truth underlying the face
we deliver in our daily lives. Each
time we choose to experience
'a next' higher level of any
emotional creation (and resulting
action in any current moment being
experienced?) we are essentially
identifying a 'next step' towards
changing a life habit/pattern which
we have identified as needing our
attention. In continuing in forward
motion we further choose to
energetically move a 'higher level
thought' into conscious action,
thereby coming to know personal
spiritual power and subsequently
'letting go' of stagnated life
energy. From our spirit we draw
strength to act on behalf of
our heart-mind. Are we living
within our hearts? Are the actions
that others and we convey the result
of an intuitive heart-mind process,

or conversely drawn from an
intellectual/ego misguided thought
process? Choosing 'a next' higher
level of thought manifesting in
action is akin to choosing alive
food over prepackaged, choosing
water over pop, choosing love over
anger, choosing a truer and truer
version of oneself, and fully
loving, respecting, and nurturing
the vehicle - our human body -
within which spirit quests for
divine clarification. Choosing
'a next' higher level of thought
manifesting inaction is choosing
life over stagnation
CHOOSE LIFE.
(8)

CONFINES OF HEART

I cowered, shy in belief of beauty
in spirit, that which carries my
body. And inside of cowering,
succumbs spirit to mind out of
control. In chaos spewing bits of
myself to the world in which I
thrive, and become. Does will break
within confines of my distracted
heart? Unable to grow in times of
denial; blossoming by way of
acceptance; healing core of
judgement. Above all else,
Love drives us. Peace Follows.
(93)

Enough Love.
There's enough love for every one.
When someone treats themselves
poorly by being mean to you,
they're all out of love,
at least not enough love inside
to give it external. So give them
love in return, because they need it
and it is our responsibility to
uphold life, not just our own.
And to not destroy it.
We don't have to love the earth
first, before taking action.
We are obliged to respect her;
love follows. Do it for yourself.
Do it for others. Do it for me
and I you. WE can get along.
Make a choice. Create action now.
There's enough love for everyone,
spread it around.
(153)

✿

(149)
rise up
fill heart
instigate change
make new choices
action matching heart
✿heart guiding action✿
✿REPRESENT✿
✿RISE UP✿
✿LEAD✿
✿

Absence of emotional congruity
inside of intellectual containment,
that shedding preconceived notions
allows intellect and emotion to work
together to assess what is true now,
our front line - who we are in
essence, balanced in our approach to
ward assessment of god, life,
each other. Emotion is our teacher.
Intellect the student.
Simultaneous.
Mind becomes emotion processed
through our human nervous system;
output through our brain via our
senses. We create, expand, become.
In doing all of this we communicate
our individual experiences with
each other - some more intimately
connect than others.

Vying for emotional truth.

Intellectual study void of emotional
input creates preconceived notions;
conclusions about who we are without
truth of our natural emotional being
given consideration. In shedding
preconceived notions by way of heart
activated mind, we experience our
basic human essence, equality by way
of being human.
Survival a right not to be
squandered at hands of others.
(87)

I'm staying here on the ground
because there is work to do. And I
was thinking, what if the only thing
 we truly know about ourselves, is
 that we exist. Everything else, is
our interpretation of isolation, for
we truly are alone until we make an
effort to connect, reach out with no
expectation of return, unconditional
 giving. Whether a connection be
  through mineral, plant, animal,
human, non-human means, we are meant
  to love. Abide together. Grow
   together. Care for each other.
  There is much to learn, in this
   regard. That I still question
how, where, why I exist shows I am
in gestation. Infant minds in adult
  bodies thinking we are smarter
  than Nature? Manipulations many.
Adult; when we figure out how not to
     kill each other for oil.
        We understand.
          (134)

Edge of Reason...Expansion of mind
propels itself from the outermost
  in life experienced. Rise Up.
        Share It.
          (148)

SOMETIMES

I saw ahead of time and the last
thing I saw I became, what I became;
greatest emotion, my bodily response
through nervous impulse ranging in
display of action by way of body
movement, sight and sound. Sense of
smell and tasted to keep us safe. A
journey through what we call
Gravity. Is God Gravity and Gravity
God? If what I am feeling is what I
become upon minds interpretation of
energy moving through, of life-force
flowing, how do I feel ***right**, now?

I looked ahead of time, and
became what I thought. Sometimes,
I feel what I am feeling, and
make choices from my heart.
(136)

***right** (adjective)
1 morally good, justified, or acceptable
2 true or correct as a fact
- according to what is correct for a par-
  ticular situation or thing
- the best or most suitable of a number of possible
  choices for a particular purpose or occasion
*New Oxford American Dictionary.

Something Ruby said set me off...

Individual in offering? Any thing is everything and every thing is all. Who am I if not but who you are as well? Upon our receipt; expressing ourselves as we are; interpretation of energy; guided by planetary wisdom, being greater energy than our known. We are connected and directed, individual in offering. The world will not come to know Peace with announcement made declaring it so. The world will know Peace when each one of us knows it to be true for ourselves, and for each one we share space with. Peace is something that grows within, and with each effort given by humans eliciting humanity; a calling forth. Where is our collective focus? Where we each are individually, combined in effects of coming together, being all forward motion happens at precise moment occurring, no more and no less, dancing in rhythm being Life.

Peace is an emotion we feel inside. Declare its existence! Promote it. Do you wait for Peace 'to happen' external to your knowledge of its making? We are independent people; living together. And what of life?

Though we may not eat it raw; it is still meat; less life left in its entirety of a-live cycle; 'death' occurring when existence transmutes, dissolving its form back into life from which we spawn. And when we experience inspiration in others, we create it for ourselves, becoming open to flow awaiting our own design, becoming one with that which creates us.

Participating.

Patience in developing equality.
Equality in human survival.
Acceptance in humility.
Connection in heart.
Equilibrium in Mind.

Opportunity for unity? There are beautiful words to wrap every occasion, as there is destructive power. Words are to be chosen, given life; love's intention flourishing in the tales we weave - stories of connection, of what saves us; our stories providing opportunity for unity to arrive. Yet how do we go about saving a world we destroy without first coming to know ourselves, how we tear ourselves apart. What do we offer in purity, untainted in our human shells?

I whispered into the night for those whose love I feel, I hope you are with us for a very long time. And just then, I realized, I was wishing for something that did not yet exist, and rather, if I enjoy each moment I have with those as they occur, I will come to know my future, our future, building together without expectation in order we may breathe our way through, guiding our way in love, binding ourselves in knowing. And so I try, to let go of that to which I cling in hopes of free expression, that love will be received. Calvin and Darby teachers of this. And in n solitude I surrender; a letting go in order to come to know what remains to build on, my part to give in unity; for this I pray. Unity belongs.

What about sanity?

I imagine the term insanity as describing particular levels of anger, bliss, or stress. And wonder, what has happened along the way to reach a place of no return? Our minds so far away from what's happening on the ground that we find it difficult to communicate with other beings in a meaningful and respect full way. Isn't that what we are? The earth and all its inhabits, a place of no return as everything moves forwards in growth, always. In a dying stage one is still alive. And death inspires rebirth to freedom, a starting over - no strings attached. Releasing hurtful emotion is a form of death inspiring freedom to live. Not be alive and exist, to be alive and live.

Is it possible to remove perception of a word's meaning out of language and feel only the sound words make - would this provide us with freedom from intellectual captivity, would it expand our hearts in order they may thrive? To solely feel. Is the music we speak our collective sense? What is the greatest harm we feel? Is it in the giving or receiving that we find our home...and when?

And what of love's insanity.

What is insanity but varying degrees of distraction experienced in personal relationship between focus of mind and focus of body; how energy exchanged between the two directs our human experience: what we call Spirit meets what we call matter, and matter meets spirit same; one not before the other;

for what we know - simultaneous they exist, and it is also said to be true, not one without the other that we know of.

Within distraction do we offer less of who we are as our attention is out of focus, ensuing chaotic communication between vessel and command. And while command is given, upon its receipt, not re-jected; given life. Life: Seed planted to be em-braced. Life force unspoken in human tongue, its calibration heart: silent in reign.

And what of the dark?

Fear keeps us alive. It feeds half of our soul with instinct of survival. Its other 180 degrees being trust, assisting in filling the circumference of who we are. They live in the centers of our bellies, fear and trust, their energy felt deep within soul; access unlimited advanced surely within tune of our greatest self-imposed limit. One cumulative world congregation - we are together.

And what of our differences? Simultaneous in form of human independence, appearing separate. Connection occurs in the joining of awareness that we grow together.

Human Rawness?

We all know it. Emotions first born of love, morphed inside betrayal, our emotional blue prints backed by our experiences. No matter how much we blame, we each experience no other but our own meaning of life. It is our duty to respect lives of others if we want to be respected and graced with life's privilege; Peace; equality full. Equality validates heart.

We sew what we reap and that which we covet blankets our hearts with fear in our distraction. We are each an intellectual and emotional blueprint; human impressions. Of what? Can we become re-learned? Do we want to?

As disease eats our human flesh, we give disease to the world. And kill it as same. World atmosphere reflection of living upon it. Does dirt in its most embryonic form care whether our skin is black, white, yellow, red, purple, green, or fuchsia? Does the earth care of our turmoil, is it obliged to? And as she roars in growth, she begs to become understood. I have, at times, felt as though my thoughts, my love, to be unworthy. Now I know what is unworthy is disrespect. Opportunity wasted every second of occurrence, filling our souls with separation, a disconnect from truth full being: energy supporting life through acceptance.

Insanity: Varying degrees of distraction. From what? How often do I bring myself back to center? Are we too far gone in raging?

Is a 'Sacrificial Lamb' one whose life is grown in moments of blind ambition? Blind ambition: another leading way; followed by external seekers in search of own. Own: opportunity welcome now. Opportunity for PEACE; seeing, hearing, smelling, tasting, touching and intuiting our way home, where heart lives. Internal knowing guiding external projection.

Becoming. Tuned to the Unit. Creating joy on the ground - keepin' love running.

What part of ourselves has not yet been acknowledged? Different and unique parts of our lives touch us deeply, at times so deeply we become one with what momentarily exits, blending with current emotional memories living closest to and in our bodies, ecstatic. At times trapped by unwilling hearts to mend our lavish wounds. Love with all our hearts, BE, with all our passion: let go toward flourish, creating beauty in our midst - BEauty in our midst; there are humans in our house.

CRY; for it is love's energy magnified. Bring it home now. Truth in heart; we see, and need each other's Rhythm...

Do our differences exist in our expressions of how we experience life? Those among humans who create steps ahead of vision in order to receive future delivery of it holding mind in ultimate state, creating dreams with action on a daily basis faith guiding. Every day an opportunity for expression of a dream. With Ruby's prodding I had to ask myself, am I living my dream? What am I doing to make my dreams come true? What are you doing to become the most fulfilled human you can be?

BURDENS RISE

Does dissatisfaction lead habitual
behavior? Eternally seeking for the
next greatest pleasure...Am I meant to
explore ego as much as it feels it has
a hold on my senses? Does my body
require that I look after its soul, to
protect it from the elements I create
of the Earth.

The weight that holds me to your heart.

Burdens rise above all
that glitters, savages roaming free.
In my mind I am a master. A god of
travesty. And with my pen I fight.
Images on a page that visit your mind
and share time creating this story.
(65)

Perhaps, Standard Notation is what we
name the use of manifest form 1, 2, 3,
4, 5, 6, 7, 8, 9; of which describe
theoretical ideas/concept. In
representing an ideal concept we use a
word called 'number'. We name the
symbol representing number 'numeral'.
The symbolism created is represented by
the word 'notation'. The ordinary
notation for whole numbers is called
standard notation - we explain standard
notation with expanded notation; we
prove 'it' within its own boundaries
and limitations, expanding as far as
the mind deliberating a proof will
reach. Math is born to prove
philosophical truths and give direction
to the meaning of life's queries and
mind pondering. It is not so much the
numeral patterns that one must try to
memorize, but rather to come to
understand and know the ideas within
the theory being proven...the numeral
patterns, if a theory presents truth,
will naturally form.
Math is a tool to be applied
by humankind in expansion of mind
as we know it to be.
Mathematics without numbers;
patterns of heart.
Patterns of spiral
coming back to self.
Drop the Zero
(56)

```
1.1................................1.1
2..2..............................2..2
3...3..........................3...3
4....4......................4....4
5.....5..................5.....5
6......6..............6......6
7.......7..........7.......7
8........8......8........8
9.........9...9.........9
8........8......8........8
7.......7..........7.......7
6......6..............6......6
5.....5..................5.....5
4....4......................4....4
3...3..........................3...3
2..2..............................2..2
1.1................................1.1
                0
1.1................................1.1
2..2..............................2..2
3...3..........................3...3
4....4......................4....4
5.....5..................5.....5
6......6..............6......6
7.......7..........7.......7
8........8......8........8
9.........9...9.........9
8........8......8........8
7.......7..........7.......7
6......6..............6......6
5.....5..................5.....5
4....4......................4....4
3...3..........................3...3
2..2..............................2..2
1.1................................1.1
                0
1.1................................1.1
2..2..............................2..2
3...3..........................3...3
4....4......................4....4
5.....5..................5.....5
6......6..............6......6
7.......7..........7.......7
8........8......8........8
9.........9...9.........9
8........8......8........8
7.......7..........7.......7
6......6..............6......6
5.....5..................5.....5
4....4......................4....4
3...3..........................3...3
2..2..............................2..2
1.1................................1.1
```

SOUL OF A BUTTERFLY

We are each
manifestation of soul,
unique in our expression of it.
One soul connecting all in essence,
feeling butterflies effect.
...elevating humanity
on wings of being;
spreading peace.
(144)

Yield to emotional commitment
toward non-tangible form,
allowing its essence to come alive
in commitment of tangible form
that supports the ideal.
Take action.
(42)

Universal flow; energy without
anger. Portrayals laced with
self-indulgence are robbing soul
from life. Some will disagree that
it's truthful while acknowledging
other side. More than half begins
to show in self deception. Toward
peace, disagreement becomes energy
of agreement; agreeing to disagree;
agreement acknowledging right to BE;
human being:being human; EQUAL.
(120)

RELATIVE FREQUENCY; RANDOM FLOW

Manipulation relished itself in
disconnect, thriving in outward
presentation; separate from truth
while disguising it so. While
action honored what seems a likely
outcome, manipulation missed
opportunity to experience now. While
most aware; mind tuned to relative
frequency; random flow; Rhythm Of
God Universal - and continues to
move toward discovery of self
telling stories of
self preservation.

May we become stripped of image
to become dressed in mindful
interaction, fresh from heart's
recognition of unity; one soulful
beat supporting another, leading
ourselves in joint venture.
ROG: Universal
(129)

Habitual behavior performed by our
body on behalf of our mind, when
exercised in extremity, enhances a
weakening of the brain muscle as the
brain becomes inactive, its muscle
becoming weak from lack of creative
use. We are each responsible for
our own actions, habitual or
otherwise in nature, by holding
capacity to prefer one thing to
another; our actions complete
through medium of choice, conscious
or habitual. One comes to trust one's
own mind in recognizing truths and
choosing action congruent with one's
truth by knowing how one's body feels
emotionally in every interaction
that it moves toward and through and
into next action with. In auto flow
of energy, that inspired of brain
waves, which sporadically create
thought upon interacting with flesh
and all it contains; the thinking,
the energetically activated part of
our brain interprets emotions we
feel cumulating movement in our body
and further applies vibratory sounds
through movement of body - what we
know as verbal and body language -
to represent external to itself a
mirror of action through the human
body, becoming external to itself
once directed action is complete.
It is a wide lens view of action we

partake, waiting to be viewed in
truth of being; to encompass meaning
of one's own mind by the shaping of
feeling through sound; resulting in
speech and body movement in
accordance to how the body feels
energetically moment to next moment
– a continuance of life until we
let go of life energy; our thoughts
departing by way of spirit form;
one's life energy passing through and
out of each cell in our body until
the human container we move about in
this world ceases to move due to
total lack of energy; spirit next
moving toward its charge.

To increase energy, we tune our
physical body through movement, and
we exercise our mind by halting auto
flow within, and in this state of
being one opens to possibility of
thinking for oneself, as freedom in
mind exits when boundaries of mind
are removed, as does exist knowing
truth within instance.

As a thought occurs, we also create
opportunity to change interpretation
of our thoughts by halting auto flow
of brain waves and newly directing
action, choosing what is ultimate
for the health of our overall being
– mental, emotional, physical – in

any interaction in which we so
engage our truth being discovered,
one enhancement at a time, moving
habitual extreme energy into a
balanced state with acts of
spontaneity; trying 'a same' thing
differently. Our habits currently
result of all life actions/choices
to now, and our expanse of awareness
of meaning of being grows by
focusing inward to our own bodies
energy, becoming enlightened in the
acknowledging of all our human
behavior, expanding in knowledge, in
truth of who we are; remembering
that all use of energy, whether
negatively or positively charged, is
conducted by action resulting of
choices of our person. Actions we
apply in accordance to our feelings
describe the state of love we are
currently expressing within our
human mode of aliveness. The closer
to truth of life, the farther from
fear based action resulting in
extreme habitual behavior in order
to keep oneself from perceived harm.
That which we know is meant to be
expanded upon until its purpose
reaches conclusion, lifting one to a
higher state of being, searching
'truest' form,
considering highest good.
(177)

It has been said it isn't
normal to know what we
want. That it is a rare and
difficult psychological achieve-
ment. My other self, suggests
in addition to this thought process
that it IS also normal to know what
we want, that when we pay attention
to emotions moving through our
bodies when devoid of intellectual
attachment; the stories we tell
ourselves to accommodate what we do
not connect with; emotional truth
not comprehended, the less conscious
part of our brain taking over as
focus diminishes – when we pay our
attention to emotions moving through
our body, we provide ourselves
opportunity for choice in awareness
to become the director of our
dreams; heart acknowledged.
(137)

On seeking truth, my friend Dave said to me..."If
we aren't seeking truth - an understanding of god,
leading to building up others in love, then we
are limited to building up self at the expense of
others."

When we focus on painful energy in
the body as it occurs, focussing on
how the pain sensations feels
minutely, we change the pattern of
energy as well. Upon focus of pain,
allowing it to be, experiencing it
for what it is, we transmute the
energy crisis into neutral behavior.
Promoting choice.
(84)

**Brains play tricks on souls, do you know your
riddle? What makes you tick behind the tricks?**

Creative flow is result of mind inter-
preting ecstatic communication be-
tween energy and the human body and
its interpretation of communication
through the nervous system directed by
spirit that we are, and accommodate.
Sensory interpretation leading way.
(76)

I have placed value on owned energy,
the kind one claims to do, be, know;
thinking removed from energy of
what's going on now, while choosing
to copy action of past, and thinking
ahead of time, to who we are
in order to exist in present.
Avoiding truth in flow.
Energy twists while bringing past
into future, and future into past;
squandering choice.
We are time travelers,
whether travelled in day or in
night. And do we steal our futures
while we dance in love of plight?
Seduced.
(69)

LOVE'S INFECTION

Feel life of love's introduction;
as we are of it; of purpose.
One's purpose revealing mystery of
life being. Love inflicted;
offerings of love infectious in
purpose.
(142)

When we think/feel/describe
ourselves as being above others in
knowledge, are we acting out of our
ability to appreciate ourselves for
who we truly are? All
that we see, all that we hear, all
that we taste, touch, smell, think,
feel and sense. We each and all
experience everything there is to
experience as one collective
conscience, one moment at a 'time',
at the same 'time', contributing to
the whole our collective conscience
growing in knowledge the more we
individually open to expansion. And
is to know ourselves, to know
others? Is to appreciate ourselves,
to appreciate others? Discovery
of equality in our recognition
of personal humanity?
Without discrimination and within
love and understanding as we are
born of love; distracted only in
illusion of separateness. As a
human race, love is the energy we
refer to as the greatest emotion in
its emitting of life force.
We are each, and all things,
manifestations of life force, of
love. Where are there differences
other than in manifest form
– in unity?
Unity strives for equality, equality
hopes for acceptance, acceptance

suggests knowledge of who we are as a
collective being apart from its
illusions. As we come to recognize
our individual illusions, and follow
through with manifest change in our
person, we open within ability to
appropriately move mountains toward
the monk; guiding, supporting,
loving, respecting and understanding
each journey, including our own,
within the sacred light that wraps
around and through us all,
connecting the infinite energy
within all, called LOVE; love in
human realm moves through
consciousness. To fully come to
know and embrace love is to move the
mountain toward the monk, and the
monk toward true nature.
(18)

Speak Your Peace; Peace Follows.
Speak Your Piece; Peace Grows.
(132)

Human illusion, in form of contributing
to human 'pain' and 'suffering',
manifests in form of emotional
attachment. We halt free flowing of
negative energy through our physical
being by way of physical tension, and,
we revisit uncomfortable emotions while
applying intellect in attempts to
release emotional discomfort. We bind
emotions within our physical bodies
with dis-ease response to that which we
do not understand or want to accept
emotionally. It is inward focus, where
the mystery of our being, the truth of
matter, will be revealed; prompting
release of negative vibes through
acknowledging feelings in response to
interactions as they occur, accepting
them for what they are on a feeling
level, and allowing the underlying
essence from that which we all stem;
love, to direct our emotional being.
In shedding preconceived notions that
we have provided ourselves with through
acts of intellectual analysis - which
bind us to physical holding patterns
- we experience equality of being;
illuminating balance of spirituality,
strengthening our abilities with
disengaging attachment - in attachment,
one reaps effects of that which one
covets by way of action directed by
emotional projection. The 'letting go'
of projected expressions of pessimistic

speculative nature creates opportunity
for recognition of exposure to
Divinity, expanding in love and wisdom,
enveloping ourselves, and those beings
with which we interact, paving way to
become truth.
(24)

Emotive Being: I wonder. Are things really meant to be hard? Is not our challenge achievable amidst respect? Honor? Compassion? Is it about love? Is it about finites that make us who we are. And when we deny ourselves, who we are - that part of ourselves we love; peaceful creation - do we deny others? For I can't love being angry but for in my mind whereupon hatred shows itself extraneous. It is not possible to feel each emotion at the same time in an intellectual state of being. Their is either/or, yes or no, me or you; required for survival. We are competitors by nature, in nature. Yet we deny opportunity to believe we can create peacefully.

I enquire of the Universe, of God, of All That Is. And is not all that exists in this Universe at this moment the greatest it has been to date, having amassed history of conscious expression. Will I hold you in my heart or file you at the back of my mind? How will I know what I want to choose? Where do I seek this information? What do I do everyday? How blind am I to the possibility that I am here for a purpose. Do we thrive amongst our competitive natures, holding space for threat of loss?

NATURE

May the nature
of who you are;
Be
your drink of choice,
Become
your drink of life,
Quenching
thirst of others.

NATURE'S LOVE

Touch the stars
of Nature's love
caressing vibe within.
See the light
of Nature's being
touching soul of All That Is.
Feel the pulse of Nature's web
and the heartbeat we each share.
Kneel heart before eternity
sampling life sublime
...within 'reality'
no one 'thing'
we can call
'mine'

Responsibility in Consequence: Is what we energeti-
cally experience as consequence directly correlated
to expectation we hold around ourselves in rela-
tionship with interaction we receive from others,
and is resultant of ones own emotional perception
and reaction to an interactions particular stimuli.
Do we hold tendency to claim victim stance, an act
of withholding truthful emotions; not expressing/
releasing energy that thwarts our bodies balance in
trinity - while blaming others for the hurt we feel
regarding our interaction with them. I imagine ev-
ery interaction we encounter is Trinity; three parts
creating particular levels of balance that outflow
in Universal proportion. Part one; energy created
within one's own energy body within an interac-
tion. Part two; energy of the 'other' receiving/giv-
ing energy simultaneous within the interaction, and
part three; being the relationship between those
interacting and our combined expression of God/
Life Force. One is not more or less responsible
than the other, for it is always a combined effort,
and responsibility of Trinity in balance rests within
oneself. Another cannot hurt me, and therefor I
receive consequence - though I can hurt myself in
untruthful awareness to my life force and its needs
for peaceful creation/expression. If expression is
full of anger, then one's expression of purpose is
in need of love's receipt - are we willing to be
in service to love, giving love freely to those who
themselves express it least? Honesty, I believe,
is expression of what is true of one's innermost
energetic value in any given moment. Do I need
to forgive another for their actions toward or in
perception against me? Is it my responsibility to

stand in truth, expressing greatest vibration of be-
ing in any given moment perpetuating same through
interaction - grateful for those times when in my
greatest good anger is what I have to offer, and
a fellow being lifts me in trinity with gifting my
'blindness' with heart's intention, stepping aside
from temptation to take on another's pain, showing
me that consequence will be what my perception of
it is in its moment of appearance.

PRIMAL PREJUDICE
Avoidance of attention.
Is spectrum
stretched in opposing direction,
while same in center where attached
in magnetic flow? Has extension
travelled away from knowledge of
what to call home at too great a
rate? Of what to call Source? Do I
feel separate because when outside
of my heart, connection becomes
ignored in fraudulent bliss?
Huminosity affected.
(47)

One all Giving, one all consuming;
character blending each; two

companions expressing the other's
need in awareness; understanding
Nature. Nature, having in all sense
observed, participates in dynamic,
love, attempting to capture life
with words; a human form of spirit.
On journey to beauty, arrogance must
also be consumed, for how does one
know emotion without two becoming
one? Without love becoming anger,
anger becoming love. The comparative
part of ourselves distinguishing
who we are, and what we know; have
become aware of; gifted of spirit's
kiss; reception granted, its words
life in energy. Perhaps they already
exist, our thoughts; being planned
ahead of time; that we may visit
this particular life. Once breath,
once human, once other? Nature: Her
sense of freedom consumed by
humanity and after consumption given
permission for it. To what extent
will Humanities need to feel
ownership grow? Will we consume
ourselves? Are we meant to? In
humans, Nature is silent, waiting to
consume so it may provide for us,
gift us with life, sustaining
herself in our image, and we
decay her; robbing her life and
stealing our own, unaware in
connection. Being of her.
(43)

If the dead could speak,
what would they say?

What once was pristine
now soured by Human Race:
We showed the world
we could conquer all,
And through our invasion
Not one may stand tall.

If God could speak,
what would God say?

You know nothing of conquering
but pittance?
What you know is shame?
What you know is blame?

What?
Life wasn't enough?

And now do you pray?
For strength to right your wrongs...
partaking.

Will you respect the dead?
And those yet to perish?

If the dead could speak,
what would they say?

Has death been in vain?
Permission to speak from the grave.
(172)

I know violence, self defacement and
soul depreciation. I know
compassion, self worthiness and
trust alongside faith.

Violence, violence is humans way,
our way, of showing what we do not
want. We fight against others to
claim what we think we believe in,
yet within fight's essence lives our
desire to not allow others to have
what they want in difference. By
fighting others to claim myself I do
not hold space for others to
believe in their own souls;
violence degrades knowing self.

In perpetuity we fight against
ourselves, exposing our nature in
action toward others. Negate
responsibility? Live in negativity
until light shines through a beacon
of heart, through awareness of
obligation to honor life, and so
ourselves and others.

Taking oneself through times of
triumph sharing value of human
spirit. Life in time creating next
highest good. One step closer.
We All Witness.
(83)

Withdrawing true spirit
so as not to give;
down playing emotions,
covering with words.

Deep circular.

Not allowing recognition
of harbored doubt;
attended to by low moral,
suffering disrespect.
Heavy?

Trust in beauty
filled with love for another.
Light?

Balance of life
between heaven and earth.
Middle?

Am I selfish
in lack of knowledge of roots?

Am I gracious
in acknowledgement?
Humble?

Do I love the earth, life?
What action do I service toward her?
Will I sacrifice?
(114)

FREEDOM

How can we, a human race, truly
experience freedom while all beings
of the world simultaneously do not?
How is it possible to experience
freedom while at expense of all that
breathes, encompassing pulse of our
planetary body? Freedom is
representational of eternal being.
Freedom imparts there can be no
captivity of all that is alive and
yet we know our human experience to
be one captive, and further still,
captive by our own imagination and
creation, by way of what we accept.
It is possible to thrive in mutual
respect, understanding, love and
support; and it is also true,
freedom is not possible while
inequality exists…that which binds
one, binds all. In freeing
ourselves from that which weights
us, and in contributing to the
earths quest in healing itself and
all that inhabits its abode, a
nurturing of balance in the spectrum
of giving and receiving needing to
occur between earth and all its
inhabitants will work toward
security of present and future
habitability.
(23)

If an opinion is one I find
contradictory, may I be guided to
not reprimand, or solicit new
behavior to replace abandoned
instinct. For it is my duty to
honor, respect, and listen to hear.

Do we subvert defensive nature into
trust by supporting another in love
and understanding, so that another
may rise out of bondage and into a
lighter emotional state of being;
free to choose as we have not bound
them to our own deluge of mania;
rather given aspects of trust to
another - free; incorporate being.

Succinct in personal need to rise
oneself.
(73)

Exalting highest good.

JUSTICE

Recognition of personal truth; a
coming to terms with the Divine
nature in each and the connection
between us all. Justice exposes the
rawness of being human while
encapsulating its cause in love, its
result manifesting in truth for all.
(49)

I woke this morning with a sense of
urgency, an undeniable feeling that
taunted patience and motivated
paralysis...an overwhelming desire
to contribute to positive world flow
has left my mind spinning - where
will I land? How do I move from
mind spin to physical action?
At times, love leaves me feeling
suspended.
(152)

HOPE
❀
...Is feeling the wind blow,
is raindrops on our faces,
snow on our tongues
mud in our shoes
and loving it all.
It is experiencing light
in every aspect of one's life;
a never-ending journey
accompanied by love
being tickled.
HOPE
is Universal love
abounding.
(48)

As humans do we hold predisposition
toward our identifiable brilliance?
Do we dare to enhance our shine when
light finds way to consciousness?
What holds thought to core of one's
life experience? What does passion
drive one to become, to risk in the
becoming? What are you inspired by,
passionate about?
Energy vibrations; feelings
described as emotions, are essential
in quest of passion. That which
we derive the most joy of propels
creation of its self, as joy is
guided by the experience of love in
growth; and love reciprocates in
being. Do we hold predisposition to
our own brilliance? Are we living
in life relationships that feed each
other in love's expanse? Perhaps
we hold predisposition to the idea
of brilliance, and thereby curb
action promoting success; as the
enormity of depth of one's potential
success is equal in depth to mind
holding vibration in 'failure';
risk of emotional loss grand.
Is manifestation of personal bril-
liance, or 'failure', representa-
tive of where one feels safety in
emotional vibration; comfort exposed
in what we gift in return to life.
(35)

Are your physical, emotional and
mental bodies aware of and
respecting your soul mind? Is your
soul mind respecting your physical,
emotional and mental bodies?
What is the combination thereof your
manifestations in synchronicity? Do
you thrive in tandem? Do you use
your intellect to react in
unawareness, or to dissect your
manifestations, exposing truth,
knowing all that is this moment?

At center point of duality
experience balance of mind as one.
At center of being – at its
innermost depth – thrives expansion
into feeling of essence of one
source; where acceptance converges
with knowledge as there are no
preconceived notions attached and no
judgments formed, simply sense of
all that is, all that has been, and
all that will be – eternity; in sum
and expansion. Our physical,
emotional and mental bodies creating
in unison with soul, sheds illusion
bound by less positive thought
processes, creating openings to the
discovery of truth, strengthening
connection to divinity.
(20)

We are
all of us.
Love and hatred.
One connected
in tendrils
of heart we grow,
distant in connection.
Love, in its growth ominous,
is wondrous. Love has no opposite
because it is free. Being of itself,
existing in harmony with all that is
Love is meant to be shared,
propagated. It is our duty, to love
thy neighbor, giving freely in time
of need. Taking while empty heart
replenishes - filling itself
while in gratitude.
How is it at all possible
to express love of God through a
human body, but for bits and pieces
making us whole. Love bursting
through silent reign.
Shining.
(121)

Every recurring upset emotion I feel, or tailor, as unpleasant emotional reaction to an interaction I am half representative of, yet while wholly in my being, begs for my attentiveness to detail of being.

And what of our world,
our emotional and intellectual
pursuits - are we balanced enough
in our systems?

We all flourish and flounder,
who teaches us to swim? What life
mechanism propels our human story
to be one that is? Is electronic
stimulation, fed by another's senses
viable? Whose view are we listening
to? Our own? What's true for you,
what's true for me? Dare I turn
inward for my own advice? Do I
claim trust enough to be led.
And to lead...

Interior focus. Feeling emotional
truth, congruency. What feeds
greatest good - lifting spirit in
recognition? Does what the world
represent feel truthful, humane?
Who represents intelligence for the
masses? We each hold voice of
Spirit.

Speak Your Peace.
What element of life, what concept
of God are you here on this planet
to uphold? Represent? Become.
Each of us playing one role of
whole. Loving our planet;
all amongst.
(127)

I wonder about love's expansion;
releasing and filling stagnation
with peace; in acceptance, happy.
And I wonder about denial;
binding heart in pressure of fear.

Alongside eternity divinity transpired.
Answer contained within,
for what else will be known.

Upheld in love given;
allowing ourselves to sing;
creating music as we learn.

Received.

Some expressed.
Some silent.
Some not here; departed,
continuing with us in spirit;
we carry on in light,
and darkness does come.

Opportunity.

Dawn not far.
Love lays low.
Desire breathing fire
into temptations glow.

Do we condemn?
Do we honor?
Do we let go?

Was Jesus, was Buddha - not of self?

Fair, Genuine, Forgiving, Human,
With Spirit.

May we choose same?

Being of them.
Human condition to know our fruition?
Will trust carry us to our destination,
balanced?

Force not necessary.
Pain guided.
Suffering devoured; its energy scarce.
Tranquillity resumed.

Exalted; enough.

Do I know that Jesus was 'Son of God'?
Do I know that God exists?
Do I believe in Buddha?
Do I believe I am daughter of God?

Our Universe grand in its expanse;
alongside, being of it.
Is it the same?
Spirit.

When will we see?
And then what will we do?
Kill each other in our deaths?
Replace life with money?

Transcendence setting mind free of
bodily glitches;our human imperfection,
why exist? And Together.

To lift Human Condition from suffering
to Equality? Loving thy neighbor in
forgiveness of self.

Respect.

Heart found when shared in offering.

Honored Presence.
Invited healing.
Taste love and fly, give birth to joy;
our creation.
Trust. Setting Freedom Bound
(119)

Upon moving through the world amongst
our fellow beings, endeavor to take
each step with an open mind and willing
heart. Each time we feel ourselves
responding to someone or something with
the action we call judgment:'judgment';
guided by personal insecurity,
misinformation; lack of knowledge,
producing fear of the unknown and
lending to creating in mind
interpretation of what the 'truth' is,
filling the gap of unknowingness with
something that our own thoughts
find acceptable, and is also a tool for
our personal growth and development -

delve deep into core, open heart and
open mind, and allow judgment and fear
of that which we choose to not
understand to be replaced with
acceptance, and further call upon
courage to emulate, by way of our very
existence, the creative mind within
which we all thrive. After all, are we
not all but expressions of one? Seek
to discover within which emotions we
manifest and of those expressions those
we experience harmony with; and choose
to live there, and grow from there;
touching all who come to visit the home
within our being with grace, dignity,
respect, and complete and full
acceptance; understanding and growing
in tune with the underlying nature of
those we encounter on our paths,
ultimately discovering our own true
nature through the illusion of
separateness. In separateness we find
our way back to oneness by contem-
plating how to once again become
personally whole. By looking inward at
our outward expressions, we encourage
discovery of the meanings behind our
actions. What we see in others is
reflection of our own nature in
particular regard. Opening of heart
and mind generates responsibility for
emotional creation, nurturing highest
good within vessel of humanimal kind.

(7)

LOVE'S WAKE

Does Spirit guide ones Heart?
Does Love flow through in asking?

Is Love's Will not ones own?

In tasting;
quenching thirst in demand of more.
Breath fueling Love's intention,
gifting Life.
Blood flows in purpose,
body alive.

Spirit pure in receipt.

Dare I live in Love?
Will it feed me?
Its power strengthening Soul.
Invigorating Mind.

Helpless in Love's Wake.
(112)

SOUL OF GOD

Absence of love once found,
shades light with cloaks of longing.
Fleshy connection ripe in the taking,
honoring rhapsody.
Desire love's nemesis, and teacher.

Love; Nature's Aphrodisiac.

For nothing as perfect as Nature
is born of anything other than love.

Anger deprives soul in tortuous
silent rage. Body aches in feelings
of rejection, and blame. Anger twists
the mind in clarity. Causes disconnect.
Separation of soul felt in belief of
humiliation, non-acceptance;
breeding hatred.
Physical revenge;
rejection in purity.
Love, lost.

Where does one look?
Are we meant to find ourselves
while looking into eyes of another?
Beautiful, in exchange of acceptance.

There is no goodbye,
no leaving of this place.
It will not be denied:
Soul of God;
Love.
(98)

Are we meant to treat everyone the same with approach to life, treating others equally in what we give of ourselves? Is it meant to be less about everyone being equal in status which lives external to our being? And is status a possible feat of exhaustion?

How I treat you comes from what I feel inside of my heart in any given moment. What we give is who we are, who we are is what matters to heart: a physical tool in addition to brain that allows us to live a human life as physiologically heart is where our systems connect - and does it matter to heart, this Center of Connection? Perhaps we are meant to exercise heart emotionally; spirit moving through our physical being: allowance to feel in support of focus.

Do we open doorways, or channels through which we 'contemplate in moments' who we are For happiness is energy that grows, as often as we choose to smile outward, and inward Laughter Heals. Love sustains.

When we are shown another's truth do we understand their communication? Does it feel truthful because truth in itself cannot be denied, at least as I understand truth to be? And does this

suggest or possibly mean that my truth
must be yours, and yours must also be
mine? Do we mate to feel this truth?
Is there such an entity,
as distraction-less thought; focus.
Ecstatic.
(71)

Ruby, how many ways do I turn a blind eye? How
often do I falter. Will I continue there. Do I rise
to occasion? Fall to opposite? Learn to dance...

One's human life, what develops with
gift of opportunity, is representative
of energy concentrations becoming
manifest by way of intention, brought
to form through action - a process of
brain filtering soul guidance, the
moving of energy in form of signals
developed from thought; showing itself
through physical movement. Physical

'reality' direct representation of what
one thinks about most, whether through
thoughts foremost in one's mind, or
thoughts underlying one's conscious
awareness, and in conjunction with
strength of emotion supporting a
current thought.

Through personal introspection we gain
insight into why we make the choices
we do, and create for ourselves op-
portunity to take action towards that
which we truly desire our human life
to express, expressing it in a way
unique to ourselves, soul guiding us
individually. How we feel about oth-
ers, what we think about others, how
we describe others, are all reflective
of what our own belief systems repre-
sent, along with displaying into view
insecurities we manifest resulting of
our soul life experience. Insecurity
negatively charges 'life lessons';
those experiences in life we have not
yet mastered and hold in fear, do not
fully understand nor encapsulate and
continue to experience negative charge
regarding until we learn to emotion-
ally shift the fear experience to a
positive energy charge by recogniz-
ing the negative energy pattern, mak-
ing conscious effort to change it,
recognizing love contained within.
(163)

We experience confidence when we are
not holding the energy we call 'fear'
around particular (inter) action. Fear
is representative of the dismissal of
our ability to securely trust one's
emotional body – it is a choice to
disregard our intuition. Intuition is
ability to trust, and further put into
action the guidance of
one's soul, one's essence.
Come to know the energy of
emotions we feel in our bodies;
speaking language of soul.
(25)

Passion dripping through, wetting
images of love; expanding knowledge,
perpetuating wisdom - potential to
wrap the world in momentum of PEACE,
gifting in return love received;
divinity unfolding.
(138)

Dreamtime

What happens when we bring our night
time dreams into our waking state
- are we then considered
consciously asleep?
(53)

❀

SILENCE   in   BETWEEN

----

somber   heart   marches
to rhythmic sacrifice
aching, seeking,
spawning
war

.

to
spirit,
home flees
face of danger,
averts deceiver ship.
and   when   one   pulls   the
trigger, own it just the same
- no more ties to blunder
not one left to blame.
but our silence.
and as yet it
hovers,
free

.

free
in silence,
free to permeate,
speaking wildly to those
who listen, changed by those
who hear. voice not seen, tongues
not fueled yet felt in twinge of peer.
each other. our silence in between.

❀
❀

The number of combinations of
'right or wrong', 'good or bad'
behavior we believe in is indicative of
how many rules we have set for
ourselves to live by. We decrease our
ability to reach our full potential by
lessoning our freedom of choice through
labeling. As soon as we attach a rule
to an interaction, we decrease our
ability to choose by half. With each
new rule added we continue to decrease
our ability to choose in quantum. By
removing the label of 'right or wrong',
'good or bad' that we place on ours and
other's action, we open to going with
the flow within our being, truly living
in freedom, not the confines we cre-
ate for ourselves by predetermining our
life's outcome with actions born of our
chosen belief system. Freedom is often
viewed, and acted upon from the stand-
point of a current social structure.
Do we fool ourselves into believing we
experience freedom from within these
types of environments, while 'non-
thinkingly' creating blindness in our
approach to life? In becoming aware
of our own restrictive nature and ob-
serving rules we create for ourselves,
we become better equipped to accept
ourselves and others, discovering per-
sonal freedom in the letting go; re-
placing rules with actions born inte-
grally, inviting divine flow as guide.
(5)

184

Provision of communal space,
within expectation of confinement of
mind, creates atmosphere conducive
to linear experience; an attempt of
capping behaviors of others
encompassed by one brand of thought
supporting dampening of spirit and
constricting living of heart space.
Sincere intention, when nurtured by
intellect though buffered from
feeling, while sincere in theory;
expands with addition of heart's
infusion. Invitation to one; and to
other, to experience and
expand awakening within, suggests
acceptance of all gifts offered;
communing individualism within sake
of unity; alleviating sameness.
Accept self; and so be it in
acceptance of others. Nurture
through invitation, respecting
journey of one, as journey of one is
journey of all combined,expanding
eternity in love's saturation;
organic in mind.
(37)

CHOOSE PEACE

As it is always darkest before the
dawn, what state of being will the
world encompass within its darkest
hour?   And what event in future
history will spur a rapid and
collective change of outlook,
causing human action on a scale so
grand it displays action opposite to
that of past negative belief
systems, creating an atmosphere of
rapid positive mind tuning,and in
so, realizing the attention of many,
and many more; paving way to peace.
What future historic event will
conscious beings lead their lives up
to, and, what have these beings
created with their lives leading up
to this event?   Is our life creation
within stress, or within peace?
A sure way to peace is through loves
intention.   A sure way to love is to
open to the giving and receiving of
it; to choose it.   Love is pure
positive energy resulting of focus
on what brings one joy.
Choose action resulting in
'feel good' energy and contribute to
present and future world peace.

(27)

Do energy motions feed through our
bodies, producing emotions we
project, presenting themselves in
what others see as our personality?
Do we share ability to nudge
emotional response as a precondition
to mindful awareness? Is it
possible? That our mind creates our
tangible self, our human body, as a
vehicle for soul to expand into
itself by way of spirit connection,
our bodies a tool used by soul?
And that each extension of itself
propels its own forward motion,
evolving in space without time;
though we keep it. Peace in our
core; zero at center, and we strive
to become aware of that which we
already know. Suffering bathes
longing within its distraction, so
as to blind memory of purpose. Do
we share ability to nudge emotional
response, provoking body-mind,
spirit and soul;
thoughts shaping potential?
(54)

While participating justification do
we sharpen our judgmental tongues,
excusing ourselves of responsibility
- adding salt to our wounds; too
much of a good thing dissolving its
own quality, in lack of truth filled
feed with which to nourish soul?
What is it of Nature we do not
comprehend, for surely we are of it?
Why do we strive to be other than
love that we are - searching beyond
our existence for answers that will
not appear because they do not
exist, except within imagination.
While we justify do we rob ourselves
of the Nature we carry,
illuminating our fears while in
exchange for love's propagation -
another sprinkle of salt; infliction
of misunderstanding and
miscommunication of all we can be.
How is it, that Nature simply is,
and as we observe her, while in our
connection with her we may also
choose to carry on in oblivious
determination; salt in excess. The
more elements we transfigure, the
further from source we run,
dissolving ourselves within our
transgressions; our external search
for understanding not to be found
as it already exists within.
Justification leading astray.
(55)

In lack of acknowledgement, neither
receiving nor giving its element,
awareness regarding within one's
environment tempts opening of mind to
gain heart's possession. And awareness
may find home there; but to the
shadows still asleep in our minds,
having not yet become, believing
external projection belongs to others.
Do we need to receive in order we may
freely give? Do we provide for
ourselves in gifting, in releasing
expectation of return? Are we complete
in exchange? And do we recognize this
gift when we give reflections of
ourselves to other life in our world?
Is it in giving to others we find
ourselves; when we learn to love?
(179)

I have been struggling with confidence, fearing arrogance and I feel grateful for second chances. Grace floats effortlessly beyond fingertips and not without striving. It's calm heart embracing faltered mind-set; creating peace with intention.

I was wondering tonight, and what I
came to realize through introspection,
is that one's life is
as great a gesture
as one's manifest intention reveals,
born of truth, caressed by doubt.
Of what do we detail? The moments
we grieve? The moments we dream?
The moments in which we are? To live
conscious birth each moment - entrapped
only in the freedom of current being
- expressing in exchange; true nature
driving potential as a parting into
whole being, inspired within truth full
motivation; and so it IS;
in the becoming.
(147)

Is there a difference, between
judgement and observation...does our
emotional stance remain unaffected
by object of attention?
Is judgement when we experience
defense? Do we pacify with
politeness while underneath turmoil
brewing in non-expression causes
energy of stress to burn the human
body, creating out of ease
state of being (diseased, ill)?
(169)

CATALYST

Feeling catalytic?
Precipitate placement.
Honor.
(133)

Love tempts us, keeps us coming back
for more; as does anger held in
reserve. To which diversion does
temptation fall? To which
temptation does spirit call?
Can love be denied, and if it can,
is anger where it lurks while in
hiding? And as love becomes more of
what it is, can it be denied but for
its own empowerment?
(14)

Deja Vu; no turning back to inside
the dream as it happens external to
dreamer. Without conscious attention;
humans living outside of creation,
forcing life. And so we die, consumed
in our seeking. Wrath felt by life in
tune with nature. In consciousness we
cling to our dependencies, taking them
with us to our graves. Our fears hold

purpose while instinct driven,
expanding out of control while outside
of body into recess of mind.
Light beams guide paths inside waves of
intuition, darkness leading astray from
heart center. Betrayal our greatest
fear? Our wholly nemesis? Wreaking
havoc in our attempts to control.
Instinct becomes lost in perspective as
we gauge what happens to us, trading
responsibility for comfort.
Catastrophic nature becoming larger
the farther from essence we travel,
bringing us physical doom; our gift of
choice squandered in face of denial.
And so we cause suffering, and weep
in our further denial that we hold
ability to change our course. Watching
our suffering with pittance of care,
survival of the masses dependent on
human greed, stealing natural resource;
devastation leads way. Gravity of hu-
man dire cloaked with image. Innocence
raged in cries of despair. And somehow
we feel shock, as if unaware;
unconscious consciousness. Our course
laid upon energy driven - we can change
our minds - we can change the dream.
Wake up. Wake me up from this night
mare. Pain too much to bare. Must we
endure more? So it seems. Yet Beauty
to be found in all, those already home
lead us there, peace full in wrath.
(13)

EQUALITY COMMON

Those times I feel lost in the
quagmire, won't you lend me a hand and
I'll lend that hand to another -
creating life of mutual freedom,
together. And is not freedom mutual in
its fullest sense? Does not mutual's
essence linger there, in home of
equality? Equality being and is food,
water, shelter, love; our basic needs
met, and sustained - money no longer
defining who we are as heart becomes
most powerful exchange.

And what of our future?

Attainment of peace, equality,
sustenance; begets peaceful thought and
sustainable action of those awarded
status of Leader of personal affairs of
others; communally, nationally and
corporately charged. Of those
entrusted, action partaken results in
development of trust and relinquishing
of fear, building human condition
through equality and assistance for
all; nurturing strength in human
ability to participate in matter
affecting the whole, while regarding
culture and geography.

Guidance toward sustenance and peace,
through one's life example prevails.
Leadership thrives in respect of

Nature; of life force; dawning ability to emit focus within balance while surrounded by challenged life circumstance; promoting peaceful interaction - leaving fear and war, raw. For fear thrives within reciprocation, breeding destruction, and in truth, consumes itself in isolation; love remaining.

Ability to lead, within atmosphere of love directing impulse, examples its support of clarity within intuitive and intellectual wisdom; promoting truth regarding Universal systems, phasing out current negative policy that we collectively agree to; that pain and suffering sold as freedom and physical power over living kind are acceptable; commendable. And that hunger exists at all. One who proclaims violence as means to sustainability and peace, in essence escalates greed, knows violence in heart and confusion in mind regarding mortality.

For how can we, a human race, truly experience freedom; trust, while all beings of the world simultaneously do not? How is it possible to experience freedom while at expense of all that breathes, encompassing pulse of our planetary body? Freedom is representational of eternal being.

Freedom imparts there can be no
captivity of all that is alive and yet
we know our human experience to be one
captive, for where there is captivity,
captors reign.

And some, we are blind in our roles, in
our responsibility and obligation of
safety for all, to commit one's life to
engaging in fear free relationship by
its promotion. In our captivity, we
are captive by collective imagination
and creation, by way of what we accept
relative to life circumstance. It is
possible to thrive in mutual respect,
understanding, love and support; and it
is also true, freedom is not possible
while inequality exists - that which
binds one, binds all. And in freeing
ourselves from that which weights us,
by contributing to the earth's quest in
healing itself and all that inhabits
its abode, we nurture balance in the
spectrum of giving and receiving
needing to occur between earth and all
its inhabitants.

And yet, while no human is above Nature
regarding sustenance,we humans continue
to breed ourselves into extinction by
way of consumption depleting nurturance
of present and future habitability.
Through recognition and utilization of
enhanced sustainability, a fostering of

success at grass roots level we lend to
expand global atmosphere regarding
community through individual
representation; what one mind
holds in truth ads but one part
to global mindset.

A Global Leader, propelled within
personal atmosphere of balanced spirit
and physical flow, inspires to know
collective energy; eliciting positive
action on behalf of humanity and
earth's environment. Acquisition of
knowledge drawn from collective truth
known to humanity at any given point
that is nurtured by peaceful intention
and is garnered with will into action
will lend to development of sustenance,
of freedom, of eradicating war;

Peace by piece ~ piece by Peace.

A twenty-first century leader of
magnitude will be example of faith in
the power of love within imagination
while emitting intellectual growth;
holding intention of successful
community; a Grass Roots Movement.
Combination of many leaders to graft
ONE Global Leader propelled in unison
with responsibility flourishing in
units will nurture sustainability.
Equality Common. Love redeems.
(162)

When we are born, is spirit
energy moving through body
pure, having just arrived from
source? Mind? And as we come to
grow into all we are, we fabricate;
become tangible existence. Creating
soul in exchange for spirit flow.
God, Universe, All That Is,
giving us life.
Can we only know what is closest in
emotional proximity to us and if so
what is beyond God? Is it infinite
because God is the last, and
therefor greatest energy cruising in
our consciousness, the one we come
to know upon departure of earthly
plane? It is the greatest pondering
of humans conscious time,
what and who are we.

Why do we exist?
(57)

When we worry about what other
people think regarding who we are
and what we 'do' with our lives, we
diminish respect for and cultivation
of our soul purpose within this
chosen life. By looking within our
own heart for direction, we feel our
way through our life purpose;
creating the life of our purpose
step by step using intuition; one's
soul directing this life's physical
manifestation by mind living in
unison with life force of itself;
creating life purpose through
discovery of personal understanding.
(19)

Is what we energetically experience
as consequence directly correlated
to expectation we hold around
ourselves in relationship to
response we receive from others, and
is resultant of emotional perception
and reaction to particular stimuli?
(150)

When we open to truths in our own
ways of being, we create space for
experiencing truths in others.
(151)

VOICES

She laced shoestrings to her heart with
bitterness; captives inside fearing ex-
posure to that which house them; mind
treading boundaries self-imposed. All
that need be honored to quell her rest-
less soul concealed beneath surface,
on edge of breaking through. As I
dreamed of all that could be, she tem-
pered my desire amongst safety, amongst
what is acceptable. I was tempted to
enquire, to contemplate: Do we pro-
tect images we create for ourselves
by choosing to believe there are lim-
ited ways to experience life? Do we
guide ourselves through habitual be-
havioral patterns, patterns of energy,
protecting our egos from feeling emo-
tional discomfort in regards to what
it is we are in blockage about? When
we hold energy blocks, are we replac-
ing our personal truths with the be-
lief systems of others? Do we embrace
our own soul values? Choosing limited
ways to experience life shrinks pos-
sibility for mind to expand, creating
narrow vision as a basis from which we
make our life choices. The more narrow
our outlook, the less energy we cre-
ate, and, the less life energy exerted.
Does life energy become minimized from
years of being expected to suppress our
truth as we individually experience it

in exchange for 'acceptable' behav-
ior? Acceptable to whom? We are born
into this world, guided by others. Do
we go through life unconsciously, fail-
ing to comprehend our true nature;
spirit residing - not realizing we are
free to let go of the binding guidance
of others, being guidance, not gos-
pel. That we are free to feel and cre-
ate for ourselves, from ourselves, free
to move forward into creation of our
own life choices, manifesting spirit.
When we experience habitual unpleas-
ant circumstances and fail to under-
stand why, do we fail to acknowledge
hearts calling? Do we accept what holds
true for our own being? Do we give
too much credence to that which oth-
ers have taught us? And in our compla-
cency to accept my responsibility for
our own contributions to life, do we
hold tendency to blame others claim-
ing victim status? Does love die a
slow death? Life vitality becomes
by choice, by seeking it, by seeking
truth behind every emotion that does
not feel 'good', or feel 'right' within
our being, we give ourselves gift of
discovery. As I dream of all that can
be, temperance succumbs in truth. As
I live, respect abided; denial grips.

(88)

FEEL-THINK

Emotions Speak;
Speak it how you Feel it.

Believe in the beauty of a thing
and it comes to you whole.
Undisrupted in courage of heart.
Fearless in desire of connection.

Trusted.

Experience of knowing.
Longing for more.

Squirming anticipation
tickles the senses
challenged by hyped intense glow.

One with rhythmic flow.

Feel-Think
(170)

We may intellectualize and
understand. How does one know?
Apply understanding towards
responsibility regarding choice,
moving toward action representing
highest good?
(154)

And Ruby, at center are we fallen? Corrupting re-
cipient earth. I wonder, does she feel rewarded,
acknowledged for housing space on other side of
dreaming? Are we compassionate beings? Honoring
that which feeds us, creating air, water, food: all
freely given, yet we price it. Is Peace full with
mercy having been received upon source arrival;
evidenced soul awakening to love's affection; kind-
ness. Sustenance creation, animals, women and
children, men, suffer at hands of humanities search
for power, its use and control.

Love wins in the end; shadows give way
to joy, their darkness brightened by
opening mind; a place where all that we
are, all that we know, all that we can
speak, touch, taste, smell, hear and
intuit becomes our tangible burden.

Burdens angst rage while living outside
of heart, burdens of joy weep in their
longing to be seen, to be heard,
to feel embraced,
to shine.

Love wins in the end. What we create
as one, and one together as all; our
essence of being living in wake of
purity. Utopian Culture blossoming
amongst unguarded hearts.

Exalted in love's pandemonium; beauty,
truth and grace stand ground. We rise
in tragic heart, our tears stained in
recognition of love's loss; how great
its space. And still, we live - to love
again. It is what we are. Love.

Do we become bits of those we spend
time with? Shared experiences blessed
by nature of co-creation?

The feeding frenzy of souls abomination
showing in greed, and lust. Unaware of
the light. Blinded by vacancy fear
produces in heart, understanding
dissolves. It is what we are. Fear.

In love we rage,
in love we imprison,
in love we wage war;
In love RAW, for PEACE.
(166)

SYMMETRY IN CHAOS

Symmetry in chaos;
fibre in threads of belief.
In what do you believe?
In what do I? Can it be same?
Is variation meant to flourish
in original tongue?
Each holding voice,
every live unit,
despite choice to not understand
different communication,
as in a Swallow's cry.
(113)

BITS OF MY SOUL

Bits of my soul
in traces of you,
does spirit move my heart?
Does longing speak to wonder?
Love I crave.
A step into time;
space nonexistent,
breath one in the joining.
Where I was once broken,
I now lay consumed,
illumined in wake of truth.
Without touch:
exhausted in desire.
(99)

Within vicinity language evolves,
original meaning lost
in transcription.

And language evolves as we do,
describing tendencies human;
scribes of old holds value new
yet lost in misconception.

our implicit implications

Save for feeling not told untrue;

our implicit implications

Does God require to know of self.
Do we search on God's behalf;
created in God's image?

Do we serve in God's regard,
seeking loves way?

implicit, miraculous

In language of voice within,
trust amongst.
(178)

Miraculous?
Do you believe in miracles?

For David...

What Does a Miracle Feel Like? I have been asking myself this question due to a recent family upset, or rebalancing, depending on which perspective I feel closet to in any given moment. Our brother David, who is only three years our senior, surprised us all with a stroke in the month of January, the 16th. This event led our family on a journey filled with anguish and love, sadness and joy, disbelief, and belief. For myself occurred exposure to meanings of life and death as deep as my soul would take me; to a truth in my being where discovery of what a miracle feels like graced my human existence, long enough for me to remember, and to share it with you. This story shares details of its nature, and I am grateful for this opportunity to express my accounting of them.

Our mother, Bev, was woken early in the morning with a call no parent wants to receive. The doctor said that David had suffered a massive stroke, and was currently hemorrhaging in the brain; that emergency surgery was necessary, that without it death was imminent, and even with it, death was probably, still imminent. The choice was easy and yet not easy at all, surgery took place while we rushed to the hospital to spend our last moments with a son, a brother, a father, to say goodbye. We were given no hope from the hands that managed David's state of being. We were told that the place in the brain where the stroke had occurred was rare, and that to live from it, and to recover in any capacity from it, was equally rare; that we would need a miracle.

I arrived at the hospital in the evening and was promptly taken to the ICU ward. As I approached a long hallway, I saw our family gathered at the other end. In an instant, that felt like a lifetime, I experienced what I imagined it would feel like to become an only child, if not for Ruby, and yet in the very next moments the depths of my soul held hope, and kept my humanness calm, holding me in a state of acceptance for David to be free to choose his direction, to decide whether life in this earthy form, was still to be his abode. I was the last of my family to arrive; I shared a few moments with them to collect my emotions, before entering the Intensive Care Unit.

Some of you may be familiar with ICU, this was my first experience. I brewed enough emotional strength to push through the large red swing doors that led me into the unknown. With each step forward David's predicament became alarming to me as the expressions of similar fated patients, greeted me with anxiety and fear, spawning cool and empty air that became my breath as I tread past their rooms, and I was rippled with sensations of dwindled life force. Though as I approached, panic dissipated in the atmosphere, and as I walked through the doorway into David's room I was enveloped with warmth and serenity. There was an expression of peace on David's face that is impossible to explain and yet I experienced it to the very core of my being. At that moment a nurse came into the room and said very loudly, DAVID, DAVID, YOUR SISTER IS HERE, and he flash opened his eyes, his slumber with source interrupted.

In ICU every life support system you can think of is hooked up to the body, keeping the human vehicle alive in case spirit of the particular participant decides to visit its human shell, temporarily, or with permanence, that is until its next departure.

In addition to life support, David had a shunt that was drilled through the top of his head and into his brain to help relieve the build-up of pressure from the hemorrhaging. The evening's memories are imprinted deeply into my mind. The next day, I sat with David for a while. I sat close, spoke gently into his ear and gazed at his face, captured by presence. I felt full of love, and peace. I felt complete; unconditional in the moments we shared.

As I sat gazing, I saw his lips move ever so slightly, and to this I LAUGHED OUT LOUD and said, I know you, you're trying to blow me a kiss, and his lips moved again. So I smiled, and I kissed him, and as we shared this exchange, the corners of his lips curled upwards, he smiled his first smile.

In those moments I was graced with a divine beauty of life, with the knowledge, and remembrance, that life itself is the miracle, in whatever form, all to give and receive equally within its own capacity, to be love.

On February 29th, David, a son, brother, father, friend, was released from the hospital and has made a full recovery. Often throughout this journey I have asked myself, is this single event of David living through this physical trauma a miracle? Or, is this single event a product of a perpetual miraculous foundation, born of life source, that we each share, that shows itself in as many different ways as there are moments? What does a miracle feel like? It feels like right now, like every breath we breathe, expanding into who we become.

Life is as one recalls it, in every
passing moment, and on the other side
of that which has, passed by in
occurrence; exists opportunity for new,
profound experience. Feel inspired to
inspire. Develop that which nurtures
health of soul in mind and mind in body
- and into mind we travel developing
human nature - with every manifest
thought in action
one's brain interprets
energy of mind passing through, using
intellect to decipher, intuition to
know, expressing our being as we come
to be it; experiencing motion, being
access to unlimited forms of human
nature; Divinely inspired,
and so All That Is.
(171)

What's inside my matchbox? It is a question I Ponder. What burns my heart. What fires me up. Where does silence come from? Where does Ruby draw her words from?

Most of my life I have been aware of my silence in a way I have not appreciated as much as I could have. Silence has been where I needed to be.

Last night I was conscious of silence, and within its conscience I recognized when I truly enjoy who I am is when I truly enjoy who people are. Whether direct, or indirect connection, we are all gifts to each other.

In silence, I experience fear of how much I feel love toward life, and how I mask those emotions with action diverting myself from the truth; that I don't have anything or anyone to be mad at, to blame, to make excuses to or for.

In silence, I hold anger in myself: being other than what I am and we are; love.

Humanism guides, at times.

I feel a greater amount of trust within myself because of our ability to share honesty.

I remember from when I was six years old, how honest friendships are, both in the keeping and letting go - perhaps pretense exists when we start to forget who we are in distraction of emotions too great to bare, or where upon too little attention paid.

The person who stands up to say "Here I AM"...and "HEAR I am" and "I will not receive others curiosity as shame (no matter how another's curiosity of who we are may be displayed toward us, with love or less than) because I recognize the truth: what belongs to me is how I feel and I know who I am, I choose to accept myself in front of everyone"... that person is blessed with conscious opportunity; recognized in spirit, truthful in soul; longing to lift others in love and in so doing, self.

Our lives are beautiful stories. We are teachers of truth, and love. And I recognize people I hold resistance toward are teachers of spiritual growth - pain and joy our mentors. That unwillingness to accept another sports flag posts of superiority.

We all endure.

For a while, I endured time blistered in chaotic brutality, relationship past that pops in and out of my life current as feelings are aroused in their and consequently my memories, my feelings now. They are meant to happen until they no longer do, being released of their ties to my heart through moments of clarity, at times spurred by another. Often by Ruby.

Last night, a memory of when I was six led me to think of a parallel incident in adulthood. As a kid, every summer I travelled to spend a good chunk of time with my grandparents. There was a boy who lived down the street that I would sometimes play with.

I was wearing my favorite green dress and we were trying to catch grasshoppers in the long grass down by the railroad tracks. I caught a grasshopper bigger than his. At some point afterward the boy peed all over the front of my dress. I stood there and watched. It was a defining moment in my life. I was not guilty of provocation. I did not understand his action, so I stepped aside to let the hurt pass for it did not belong to me.

I watched from outside of myself.

I stood my ground.

My abuser urinated on me as well. He threatened me into standing in place to receive his disrespect. His distain. Underneath the terror I felt speechless grief for the pain one must feel to be on the giving end. I was conflicted in difference of passion and torment, lost in between until I saw through, and reached for a lighter way of being; trusting that I was ok. That I would survive him. That my heart may be affected in order my soul protected.

I observed.

After some thought, I recognize that perhaps I've given little sound to my voice as I have needed to live inward to heal from wounds I have bore, and retain. I am a refurbished human. I have been defiled, humiliated, hated.

And that was how he showed his love because that was what he was taught, and learned love to be. I believe we all seek it. I cannot fault him for it. I cannot condemn, nor condone. My resource is forgiveness; allowing myself to be ok with the fact that I loved this man deeply, in the best way that I knew how to love at the time. As did he. As do we all I believe. And no matter how much I want to believe that he should have known better, I cannot rely on my interpretation for if he truly did, he would not hurt another.

What I have experienced so far offers that Love is something we choose - acceptance of another. It is not fair for me to judge, and yet I have when I offered no solution. Nor hope.

I was patient in receiving my beatings, I endured without protest, without fighting back, I accepted his position, not solely because of fear, and partially because I loved him.

I have used fear as an antidote to love. I've feared anointment in those moments I was not hating him.

And, my abuser was mean, and scared. My plot assigned professional descriptive depiction similar to that of a prisoner of war; tortured mentally, physically, emotionally, verbally, sexually, and spiritually.

And, my pain is real - who knows what all I have
stored in hopes of revisiting next life, too emotion-
ally endowed to visit now.   And so I carry on.

Do I stand in judgement when I sit
here offering merit to but one per-
spective?   Does not each as well
hold within itself its opposite,
its outermost reach from what it
is now and amongst   all its
in-betweens?   Opposites ground-
ing purpose within range of all op-
portunity.   Each to be respected,
all managed within love's intention.

(44)

Ruby believes that people hold ability to choose
which emotion to accommodate and resonate with
at any particular time.   That we may choose to
get to know our emotions, how and when we use
them and with what purpose in mind.   Objectivity
resides.   And within observation, emotion; the com-
ing together of how energy in our body feels when
using intellect and heart center in unison, displays
nature.   That combination of what the mind thinks
and what the heart feels at any particular time,
produces energy specific to its union; resulting in
e-motion; energy-motion: all entity; spirit and body,
guiding the other through processing knowledge of
self.   Within our sense, human scope.

Ruby would ask me: do we use human relationship
within this scope in order to discover our essence?
Do we get stuck in relationship thinking it is what

life is about, that it is where we will find our happiness and sense of completeness, external?

Much deeper than what is on the surface of ability of the human mind alone to satisfy the cravings of love and union we seek in partnership with another's soul, indeed is our own relationship with the universe that is being displayed upon culminating of energy manifesting by way of body and mind.

And in any given moment, we glide, and, we flow wholly into forward motion; body and soul physically awake and mentally alert, self expression full.

Ruby and I both believe, that one of the greatest offerings we can give and receive is contained within and filters through our hearts.

That as angles before us, angels come after, taking our place in departure, as we depart for home; wholly in heart. And in patience, and silence, as I come to know heart, emotion longs to be heard in the silence it hovers and so appears as words on the pages my fingertips seek.

...and in trust, freedom bursts. No remnants of a Ruby red apple found, but for spirit.

I think of emotional pain, the kind I have experienced in life, and I remember, both are inside myself: the joyful bliss of a summers kiss, and deathly blow; a grieving process where outside of self I tell my self stories, as similar to moment as focus in distraction allows.

What I want to experience is a greater sense of connection. It is to share in friendship. To dance in the moonlight and gaze at the stars. To feel happy. To hold new life. To surround personal experience with those joyful in order to fully experience joy, and with those hateful, to understand why...

...why do we experience aggression toward each other?

I believe we are all of the same, when it comes to spiritual inheritance. And so I ask, why does empathetic indifference exist?

Does willingness to look the other way perpetuate atrocity? Does the clubbing of a baby seal, the skinning of a cat, the picking wings and legs off of bugs, the sawing of antlers, the caging of animals, the boiling alive of sea creatures, the spilling of oil into our water source, the beating of a child, the rape, torture and murder of another living being, and hunger, all share similarity? Life source?

How does one come to choose to love one thing, and yet reject, and perhaps harm another?

Love permeates - how do we halt its flow while being of it? Imbued superciliousness? Supersize me outta here: the embarrassment, the shame. Must we continue to embrace madness in face of ourselves?

May we earn love, and may we speak freely? Following is the last letter I received from Ruby.

It was placed in the kitchen cupboard, where morning ritual lives. She seemed frustrated, distracted... she wrote of her love for animals:

I am beginning to sense why one smells
the rose while another plucks it.   For
I am both.   Any animal will prove this.
For they know no human existence ex-
cept for their experience of who we
are. A kind hand, one that strikes.
In love, humanimals flourish.   And when
given anger, hatred, animals fear
not us, but succumb in love's loss.
Drowning in oil and other such commodi-
ties of greed. Do we offer fear when
having travelled too far from heart,
our minds expanding so far that we
are not able to remember who we are?
Disregard for what connects us led
in anger, betrayal and blame? Acting
harshly, and speaking blindly. For ac-
tion and words are emotive; meant to
be given with kindness, compassion,
respect and nurturance. Animals love
with no condition in order for us to
see ourselves; they are mirrors to our
soul. Animal soul: words not distract-
ing emotion; free to be heart, to love
unconditionally. Do we give heart away
when we engage control of expression?
Speaking within rules, conforming...
(174)

This morning, I wrote Ruby a letter:

Dear Sister Ruby,

It's our birthday today and I need you. Where have you disappeared to? I've been looking for you this morning. There's a story I want to share with you. But how do I tell it? It's been coming to haunt me. I have much to confess and questions to ask. I have a secret to tell you, meet me under the apple tree.   Meet me there so I will know what to look for, in search of beauty; you are my sister and I love you. Perhaps we can walk to the forest edge. You never know, we may get a glimpse of Hazel.

Being it's our birthday, I've been collecting your prose in this book, and it is my gift to you. Happy Birthday, Ruby!

Love, Asil.

...Hazel is a sister from another mother. Our family is large, and some live in the forest. Perhaps we will spot her later today. It wouldn't surprise me, many have been coming out of the cracks and crannies. Aside from birthday preparations our village is abuzz with anticipation!   There has been talk of a Revolution. A grass roots movement. There is much to celebrate.

I am guessing talk of Revolution is what led me to the dream I awoke to this morning. I dreamt that flowing from me was toxic water. That I was polluting the earth. Blood flowed as rhythmic seas. And clots of ill intention burst into dancing starfish, being born of our plight. Humanities suffering birthing soul of God, Universe, All that is: to begin anew, to dance with the starfish.

And then I remembered, we are all family, courageous hearts carving waves through passage of time. In my dream, I thought I was Ruby and I wrote the following poem:

Dance of the Starfish

I dreamt of a hemorrhaged sea,
flowing freely from the depths of me.

And the starfish danced in their delight,
born once more and within their sights...

...a race of be'ing who belong,
singing pulse of Nature's song.

As the starfish danced in their delight,
frolicking free of human plight,

I dreamt of a hemorrhaged sea,
its toxic waste gushed forth of me.

And as I stood and watched my peril,
I wished I had of...

...danced with the starfish.

And then, I gave birth to a boy. He was throwing Starfish back to the tides, holding time in sense.

He was whispering to source. There was an old man standing nearby, and as the man turned to walk away, he heard the boy whisper, 'There lives hope in the anguish humanity creates. Unity resides in our discovery. At home in Spirit.' Something in the man began to quiver, he clutched at his heart, wretched his innards and prayed for mercy. The pain too much to bear.

As the boy continued tossing Starfish, the old man, through his torment, saw opportunity in choice yet did not know if he bore the strength to change. So he clung to what he knew, mumbled to himself as he shuffled away without risking to try. And so his pain continues. When I awoke this morning, I knew that I had to tell Ruby my secret. I have held it for too long.

Perhaps my conversation with Ruby last night also spurred content in my dream. I had asked Ruby her opinion of the talk of Revolution in town and she said to me, "There is Jesus in the Devil, and so the devil seeks man; replenished abolition stealing soul from creation. And as humanity seeks, to remember, the wicked wage war and the saintly cower, forgetting their power of VOICE. To rise up, to speak loudly, to be peace full CREATING PEACE for at heals of suffering beauty nips, purchasing hope with light remnants; bartering glorified dreams for sacred intention, setting self-imposed limits toward freedom; suffering, at hand of gatekeeper. Precedence set me, free."

I placed the letter I wrote in one of Ruby's favorite

places, under the ruby red apple tree. Ruby visits this particular tree each day. She claims it to be full with God's essence, and universal truths. I will wait for her there, after celebrations. I want to give her this book today. You are welcome to wait with me, and if you wish, help keep an eye out for Ruby.

Following is a list of my rants and ponderings, as well as a list of 'PROSE TO PONDER' that contains titles of the numbered prose from Ruby, and which pages they are on:

Asil's Voice

PAGE #'S:

2-10
12-17, 18
21, 23-24, 26, 29
34, 37
40-41, 43-44, 48-50
54, 57, 58
60, 65
71-73
80-81, 89
91
109-116
124
137-142
151, 152, 157
159-160
170, 179
188
201, 205-208
209-216
217-226
228-231

Buddha (101)

(p30-32) Sitting, With Peace (1)
(p33-34) One Soul (2)
(p10-12) Essence of Being (3)
(p30) Be Integration (4)
(p183) Create Within Conscious Intention (5)
(p100-101) Illusion of Judgement (6)
(p174-175) Seek To Discover (7)
(p131-132) Choose Life (8)
(p126-127) Heart's Desire (9)

(p62) Energy of Love (10)
(p73-75) Energy Motion (11)
(p61) Taunting of Mind (12)
(p190-191) Unconscious Conscience (13)
(p190) Love's Empowerment (14)
(p41) Worry (15)
(p51-52) Energy Flow (16)
(p56-57) Endeavor (17)
(p154-155) Monk Down From The Mountain (18)

(p197) Purpose (19)
(p169) Connection (20)
(p35) Ode To Love (21)
(p46) Life Direction (22)
(p165) Freedom (23)
(p156-157) Become Truth (24)
(p181) Mind-Body Connection (25)
(p158) Nature (26)
(p185) Choose Peace (27)

(p96) Denial (28)
(p122) Energy Flow of Now (29)
(p98-99) Not Guilty; Peace Full Wrath (30)
(p102-103) Peaceful In Wrath (31)
(p87) Birthing (32)
(p129) Anguished Euphoria; Peaceful Wrath (33)
(p117) Thought Creation (34)
(p168) Predisposition to Brilliance (35)
(p58-59) Love Reciprocated (36)

(37) Love Saturated (p184)
(38) Emotionally Translated (p20)
(39) Appeal from A Dying Animal (p44-45)
(40) Beyond Paralysis of Mind (p84)
(41) Waking of Soul (p105-106)
(42) Commitment (p146)
(43) Possibility (p160-161)
(44) Love's Intention (p213)
(45) Grace (p89)

(46) Mercy (p108)
(47) Primal Prejudice (p160)
(48) Hope (p167)
(49) Justice (p166)
(50) Quicksand...'Aint' So Quick (p128)
(51) Beauty Shines (p93)
(52) Harmonies Call (p94)
(53) Dreamtime (p181)
(54) Potential (p186)

(55) Justification (p187)
(56) Mathematics (144-145)
(57) Why? (p196)
(58) Womb of Soul (p18)
(59) Mind Body Translation (p19)
(60) Harmonies Consumption (p21)
(61) Infinity (p21)
(62) Linger Longer (p68-69)
(63) Silence in Between (p182)

(64) Containment (p130)
(65) Burden's Rise (p143)
(66) Vibe (p63)
(67) Kindle Soul (p123)
(68) Triathlete (p120-121)
(69) Seduced (p153)
(70) Potential's Peak (p130)
(71) Ecstatic (p178-179)
(72) Love's Intention (p46)

(p166) Politics of Being (73)
(p23) Physical Genius (74)
(p51) Association (75)
(p152) Sensory Interpretation (76)
(p76) Drink In Desire (77)
(p76) Love Expanded (78)
(p58) Mind Chatter (79)
(p22) Recipient Vision (80)
(p25) Harvesting Heart (81)

(p65) Heart's Content (82)
(p163) We All Witness (83)
(p152) Energy (84)
(p42-43) The Reaping (85)
(p117) Freedom Lives Here (86)
(p134) Tangible Nature (87)
(p198-199) Voices (88)
(p75) Impatience (89)
(p57) Heart Filled Desire (90)

(p107) Peaceful Intention (91)
(p50) Identity (92)
(p132) Confines of Heart (93)
(p47) Effective Connection (94)
(p28) Dare I (95)
(p25) Growing Life (96)
(p27) Brilliant Being (97)
(p177) Soul of God (98)
(p203) Bits Of My Soul (99)

(p66-67) Choosing (100)
(p54) Emotional Literacy (101)
(p17) We Are All of Us (102)
(p125) Peace Full In Tension (103)
(p63) Image Up (104)
(p70) Document (105)
(p90) Whispering Loves Intention (106)
(p36-37) Zero Objective (107)
(p55) Does Soul Know My Name? (108)

(109) Heart of Soul (p53)
(110) Emotional Observation (p29)
(111) Expectancy Delays (p88)
(112) Loves Wake (p176)
(113) Symmetry In Chaos (p203)
(114) Am I Selfish (p164)
(115) Change Me (p118-119)
(116) Tainted Replica (p75)
(117) Feeding Ourselves (p86)

(118) Waves (p79)
(119) Setting Freedom Bound (p172-174)
(120) Soul Paper : Self Deception (p146)
(121) Love's Silent Reign (p170)
(122) Us (p92)
(123) Material Stimulation (p38)
(124) Gravity (p124)
(125) Surfacing (p67)
(126) Love IT Change Our Light (p94)

(127) All Amongst (p171)
(128) Strings of Thought (p82)
(129) Relative Frequency; Random Flow (p147)
(130) Chemical Love (p77)
(131) Anguished Euphoria (p68)
(132) Peace (p155)
(133) Catalyst (p190)
(134) Gestation (p135)
(135) Human Vehicle (p28)

(136) Sometimes (p136)
(137) My Other Self (p151)
(138) Passion (p181)
(139) Thoughts? (p124)
(140) Inhalation of Spring (p95)
(141) Subliminal Support (p39-40)
(142) Love's Infection (p153)
(143) Love came round to find me. (p96)
(144)   Soul of A Butterfly (p146)

(p95) Growing Radiance (145)
(p78) Feel What You Think (146)
(p189) In The Be Ginning (147)
(p135) Edge Of Reason (148)
(p133) Rise (149)
(p197) Consequence (150)
(p197) Truths (151)
(p167) Suspended In Love (152)
(p133) Emotional Pandemic (153)

(p201) Soul Navigation (154)
(p94) Permission to Freedom (155)
(p78) Moments of Passion (156)
(p88) Stature (157)
(p86) Lady Shakesphera (158)
(p61) Moments of Connection (159)
(p62) Distracted in Ritual (160)
(p63-64) Soulless Keepers & Heartfelt Souls (161)
(p192-195) Equality Common (162)

(p179-180) Contained Within (163)
(p83-84) Thrust (164)
(p104-105) Soul Manifestation (165)
(p201-202) Raw For Peace (166)
(p126) Trust (167)
(p50) Beings In Universe (168)
(p189) Out of Ease (169)
(p200) Feel-Think (170)
(p208) Human Nature (171)

(p162) Permission to Speak (172)
(p97) Resident Motion (173)
(p216) Title-less (174)
(p158) Nature's Love (175)
(p85) I Wonder... (176)
(p148-150) Habit (177)
(p204) Trust Amongst (178)
(p188) to Give and Receive? (179)
(p116) About Mercy (180)

(181)   The Gate Keeper (p1 and p219)

CHAPTER ONE, Book Two

It has been many months since our birthday, I never did see Ruby that day. She has gone missing. So much has transpired since then. Birthday celebrations came to an end, talk of Revolution continues. Grief arrived. Heart anguished. Shortly after our birthday, I moved close to the lake, just outside of our village, seeking solace.

In this moment, I am sitting under the apple tree, still watching for Ruby. And as I wait, mind rambles on...

There is a creaking in the distance, a rattle of rhymes. I wonder if it's Ruby, trying to reach me. I have not been able to sense her. I realize now, she is not coming back and that I too, shall leave. I must find my way, my own voice. Some have said Ruby and I sound alike, at times. We are twins after all, though I have become frustrated, at times angry and tired of relent. And will you think I am crazy in the ramblings that follow? And am I, crazy? If you do not understand me, does that make me insane, does it make one that judges, unaware? Shall I change who I am to accommodate? Compromise soul.

Is Ruby Dead? I wonder, does where we come from feel death? Mourn our departure having itself come from somewhere in birthing us. Does what we collectively call spirit, name it as we shall, something greater or nothing at all, does IT need a name? And when we name IT, why do we then go to war on ITs behalf? Fighting amongst ourselves in ITs honor, as if killing, starvation, and superior control is what IT had in mind.

God, Universe, All That Is, even atheism is a belief in something, for if nothing exists, how can there be perception of it? And is varying degree of physical pain reminiscent of unsettled nature.

far from peace, unbalanced in material body, spiritual body, in all form. How do I release this anger?

Death, will you take me? My vengeance upon tainted soul. Will anger spare me...

In what ever form, in which ever way, here we are. Fighting over the right to live or die, while killing each other. Supporting war, hoping for peace. If you want peace and speak nothing, if you share silent agreement, it is time to step up. To speak out. Appear. In our silence truth loses voice. Those who seek to control gain power in the giving of ourselves away. And they don't have to take it because we eagerly give, trusting politics, defacing heart and intuitive nature.

People have the power. I feel power in the forest, it has been calling my name. And I, I will die on this journey. It is written. And for this, from now I live alone. I'd like to tell you the story. Of how it comes to pass. How threat of peaceful existence grew itself an army. How for a time it snuffed heart to silence acknowledgement of love, compassion, unity. How grief stole my soul and forced hand of faith. If Ruby were here I would ask her if she believes that essence of trinity exists if we allow it. Come to know it. Not whether we have, in the past attained it. Acting now as though something has been lost. Copying past in our grudges and future in our past.

Are we here to discover our hearts? Has mind ventured too far on it's own? It can be said that mind destroys. And this beings heart becomes foul in desecration, and still it heals by heart of another. Heart emissions? Chord struck? Perhaps it is my own twisted soul that torments. And still a question remains, do I want IT? Peace. If there is to be a devil, its heart acts upon fear of unknown, killing community different from own. And what I fear most, is that I will not come to love you, holding damnation as savior.

Whom among us will walk? Whom will stand? And oh the pain of love once lost to distancing of self. Do I quell longing by creating terms of death, departure in calls of despair, grief, loneliness. And yet a single loving touch holds the hand of heartache, so it may come to pass, to be replaced with sense of acceptance, acknowledged cohabitation. In the end there will be no silver bullet for this heart, it died such a long time ago. Just a flick and I will disappear. And once more, may mercy come to greet me filling soul with blessed love. For I will come to die, and yet, I shall live through heart of young, and on my side, reconstituted time...

...and as Starfish, shall we dance?

There is a story I must share. Will it be you who reads it? Some move sweetly to death, others must battle to die. In the end, will we see each other? Do my ramblings make sense, to you?

Ah, sweet life. As anguish shifts into lower energetic frequency, longing for it grows last connection shared, promoting more of itself until mind recognizes shift in energetic neural matter; oxygenated thought waves flowing synapse, expanding. What is out of balance within energetic value? Energy we agree to call regret? Selfish gain or philanthropic nature. Is there an end? A new beginning? Will there be PEACE. What is the passing of spirit from existence, the one we know. If I had made different choices, how would my life look? What kind of spirited body would I acknowledge? What determines love? And vengeance grows; magnetic attraction gaining on self devours. Consuming beyond attrition. Do I sound bitter? Do I need to let go? Perhaps, perhaps not, for measurement of time will do this for me. It is PEACE I seek on this plane. I ask again, am I insane?

At times, it feels for my sanity I must find Ruby. And Calvin and Darby, where are you? I remember you when I focus on how I felt when I was with you. And now, I must learn to feel you in a different way. To allow myself to continue on. To live life for today. To embrace spirit of another. For do we not all want to be seen in the end, be acknowledged? I do not know what the future holds. Sure, I can visualize a dream. It is that faith guides heart. That trust binds soul with mind. That unity embraces conscience.

Catch me when I stumble, for it will hurt you more than upon myself, will allows. As Ruby says 'lift me up when I am down, for my heavy heart will bring you down as well, oxygen an embryo, we, of it.' See you in dreamland, Alice. Perhaps we are already there?

Early one morning I was walking in the meadows, I recall coming across one of Ruby's prose. It was dangling from a dew sprinkled web. It was prose #143. I remember thinking to myself that it felt out of sorts. Her train of thought left open. I haven't thought of it again, until now.

This evening, I am tossing Ruby's book into the void of the forest, not daring to yet cross over. I trust upon the stars it will reach her, for stranger things have gone on there. Elders in our Village warn that mind becomes lost there, in the forest. And lately, I have been accused of insanity. Am I losing my mind? Is it sanity I seek? I will begin my search for Ruby tomorrow morning, at the trail to where the forest begins. Will you venture with me?

CHAPTER TWO, Book Two

She can hear them, somewhere, bells ringing, rapturing sound, capturing longing; so as to quell heart enough to fill itself with will to carry on. Heart reaches for heights greater than last achieved, creating peaks and valleys. On the down slide to ground is where heart empties self, love having soared beyond measure; developing need to recognize itself through conscious loss. Harmony awaits those willing to once more climb love's myriad path. Such is the ebb and flow of life; to strive for peace, battles fought in self defeat. Love is what remains making conscience bearable and peace, attainable. And so she searches for IT, does Asil...

...As water flowed freely in front of her, waves of inhibition silently washing the shore, scattering hope and nurturing healing, it had became her custom. Each Sunday since their deaths, Asil ventured across the street and down to the beach: chair in one hand, journal and steaming mug in the other, still cozy in her pajamas and housecoat, faux fur lined hat secured on her head and puffy winter shell wrapped around her to seal her bodies warmth – she searched there for remnants of her heart.

Darby had gently nudged her inside of her dreams, to go and hover at the water's edge. As she sat there staring out over the landscape, a boat skimmed by, rippling waves of sound. Across the way, motorized vehicles carried souls to and fro. As she warmed her hands on the steaming mug, condensation escaping her breath, she wondered, where does love come from and why does a plane fly overhead? The ticking of the engine drowning out Nature's vibe and yet somewhere in the distance, across the water's expanse a rooster crows, a dog barks and all feels right, for a moment.

The snow is covered with bits of tree and animal prints beg patterns of discovery.

As Asil looked up to the sky, lavender blue surrounded all below it, poking through puffs of cloud. The mountains felt enormous to her, on the other side. Their shadows large, pebbles small beyond the snow, rinsed upon the shoreline, just inches from her feet. It's been several months since they passed, transitioned back to spirit. Asil was lost for a time. And while her heart felt broken, mind twisted faith, disconnected her for a while. I felt this, it pierced my heart as though it were my own.

As she took her last sip she resolved herself to walk back up to the village, to sit beneath the ruby red apple tree, searching for yet another sign, waiting for snow to melt and apples to drop.

My name is Lucita. Ruby has gone missing, I am not sure to where and Asil, she searches for her. Asil is of my heart and no matter where I am I feel her, sense her direction, yet I am blocked to her, as Ruby is blocked to me. Asil is leaving tomorrow to look for her, from where the trail into the forest begins. I will not share physical space with Asil on her quest, though I will follow her, as I too, seek Ruby. Asil carries with her a secret, one that longs to become known. Just this morning, I heard rumor of a book being passed amongst forest dwellers, and then I came upon it. And here it is in my hands, my pen imprinting its will. It is said that those who come across it, join in search for what has become lost to them. I know I am meant to release this book, having now held it in my possession, its destiny to reach the hands of Ruby. Though something inside of me clings to its departure. Perhaps I will hold it for just a while longer. The time will come to set it free – it will lead us, Asil and I, to the gem we seek.

As Asil turned from the beach, the lake spewed forth a ferry boat named Osprey, beings aboard. And aren't we all?

Will you join us? At the trail to where the forest begins...